T0283842

Praise for *Snapshots Sent Home*

"JT Blatty's *Snapshots Sent Home* is a sweeping and illuminating account of what it means to not only fight as a soldier or a civilian combatant but also to document war—to make photographs and record first-person accounts of lives lived on, or in close proximity to, an ever-evolving series of frontlines. ... Blatty's memoir kicks into gear in the weeks following 9/11 with her service in Kandahar, and it never stops as she takes us from Afghanistan to Iraq to the Donbas and Kyiv in Ukraine and back again. Her powerful, engaging narrative travels in and out of time, forward and back, to create an interwoven and kaleidoscopic portrait of her experiences, and those of the people she meets and grows close with along the way. These are lives caught up in the crosshairs of tremendous political and historical shifts—and Blatty shares her and their stories with immediacy, honesty, and depth. She has a gift for conveying a sense of place and people that is usually only arrived at by being there: the men and women who people this book are richly and vividly drawn, like characters in a good novel. As Blatty discovers her purpose, we learn more about what it means for her and her comrades to fight for home and nation, sovereignty and freedom. *Snapshots Sent Home* is a challenging, revelatory, and important book—one that takes us far beyond, as Blatty writes, the 'disconnected world [of] reports and skimmed-over news headlines.' This book is a rare and moving testament to the ties that bind those who experience war and its ongoing, lasting effects."

—Alexa Dilworth, independent writer and editor; former publishing director and senior editor at the Center for Documentary Studies at Duke University

"Through a series of dispatches, across several frontlines, former US Army officer turned journalist, JT Blatty weaves a wholly unique and timely account of life during wartime on Ukraine's eastern front. Sometimes humorous, often gut wrenching, lines like 'I went to take a shower. I stood there ... crying and picking pieces of my friends out of my hair' stay with you. Under the blanket of slow terror that hung across Ukraine leading up to Russia's invasion, Blatty finds love on the other end of her camera lens, and perhaps, part of herself. Like so many of her fellow veterans who fought in the post-9/11 wars, a crisis of conscience formed when the dust settled. Questions nagged.

And much like the American volunteers drawn to the Spanish Civil War, Blatty feels herself pulled into Ukraine. A war without moral ambiguity. A war where the line between good and evil is more clearly drawn."

—James McGrath, former bureau chief, Gamma Presse

"Blatty's unparalleled memoir gives readers a glimpse of what it is like to be on the frontline. There's only the universal truths of war and conflict. The lingering thoughts, memories and moments afterward that stay with you. *Snapshots Sent Home* captures these moments perfectly for those with an eye on history."

—Robert P. Ottone, author of *The Vile Thing We Created* and the Bram Stoker Award-winning novel *The Triangle*

" ... *Snapshots Sent Home* is an intimate, finely-written memoir about the truths and realities shared by soldiers everywhere. Moving between the author's experiences in Ukraine, where she lives and works as a photographer, and before that in Iraq and Afghanistan, where she served as a US military officer, Blatty ruminates about the nature of comradeship, patriotism, longing, loss, life and death; memory and love. 'Butterflies on fire' is a phrase that makes a debut too, but you will have to read this devastatingly moving book to understand its meaning. *Snapshots Sent Home* should be read by anyone who cares about what we do on history's battlefields, and about how we process what we have done afterwards. This is a lot more than a book about snapshots. And JT Blatty is a lot more than a photographer and former soldier. She is a helluva writer too, and I am certain that what she says here will stay on in readers' minds for a long time to come."

—Jon Lee Anderson, staff writer, *The New Yorker;* author of *Che Guevara* and *The Fall of Baghdad*

SNAPSHOTS SENT HOME

From Afghanistan, Iraq, Ukraine —a Memoir

JT Blatty

Elva Resa * Saint Paul

Audio excerpts transcribed and translated by
Anna Kyselova, Vera Golubkova, and other volunteers.

Front cover photo by Юлія Толопа.
Back cover author photo by Dmytro Lavrenchuk.
Cover design by JuLee Brand of Design Chik for Elva Resa.

Library of Congress Control Number: 2024930107
ISBNs 978-1-934617-81-6 (pb), 978-1-934617-82-3 (ebook)

Printed in the United States of America.
1D 2 3 4 5

Elva Resa Publishing
8362 Tamarack Vlg, Ste 119-106
St Paul, MN 55125

ElvaResa.com
MilitaryFamilyBooks.com

*To the veterans of all wars
and to all who fight for change*

CONTENTS

Author's Note

I NEVER BELIEVED IN THE INTENTIONAL PHOTOGRAPH, at least not in the journalistic world, when trying to capture the truth. Years of working as a photojournalist had taught me how false an intentional photograph could be, in the days of handshake photos for FEMA, politically motivated assignments for the *New Orleans Advocate*, and being pushed by *The Weather Channel* to exploit "swamp people with alligators" after Louisiana tornadoes. That's why my decision to make portraits of Ukraine's 2014 volunteer soldiers of the war in the Donbas went against every grain of my being. It was unfamiliar territory, to stick them in front of a black blanket and to use a flash, of all things, something completely foreign to me—creating light instead of seeing light in a moment. I was suddenly "making" a picture instead of taking a picture, as some of the most educated fine art photographers always liked to emphasize. A studio type situation that prompted the best of posing, to encourage an appearance of how they want the world to perceive them, or how the photographer wants the world to perceive them, instead of being seen as who they are.

I never believed in the intentional photograph. But even within these intentional portraits, I found a way to capture the volunteers in the most non-intentional moment. When they were looking at me instead of the camera lens. When their eyes conveyed a moment of truth that was first revealed in their voices during the hours of audio recordings. A moment when a stranger can look at their portraits, listen to their voices, their stories, and maybe find someone not so different from themselves. A moment when a soldier of any war might identify with a familiar tribe.

My knowledge of the fine arts and technique isn't a strong point. It doesn't enter the text of artist statements I'm required to write for exhibitions, the wording of grant applications or pitches for publication where the "process" of making art is a critical factor. Even my studio situation in Ukraine, where I capture their portraits after recording their stories, isn't a studio. Just a black blanket draped inside flats all over Kyiv, hung with double sided tape or roped onto old Soviet era lamps, or hooked onto random sharp objects in warehouses or bunkers in the Donbas, or even tied in between two forest trees on the front line.

Some photo editors reviewing my work critiqued my use of the flash by the lack of consistency in the white balance. The tones always varied depending on my location and the tone of natural, ambient light coming through that day. The same kind of photo editors skipped over the excerpts from the volunteers' audio stories. Because the volunteers, the war in Ukraine, it just wasn't timely or relevant for them to publish or to award American grant money. These soldiers weren't a trending headline, they weren't fast-paced news, and I wasn't on assignment.

When I started the project in 2018, I didn't have a posting to recruit participants. There wasn't exactly a set of criteria they had to meet, only that they had to be part of the 2014 movement, and I preferred not to interview commanders, highly published "heroes," or people who wrote to me asking to be part of the project. It wasn't because I didn't think they had a story to tell. It was just too intentional, too predictable, too much of an assumption about what I was trying to capture. They didn't realize that one day, I'd cross the border and interview the other side. One day, I'd interview veterans of all wars. Because the story wasn't only about preserving the volunteers and what it meant to fight for freedom. It wasn't only about educating the world about the present, showing that there was still a war in Ukraine and that there were people still fighting for independence in the twenty-first century. I was searching for a story that could one day be stripped of flags, uniforms, borders, and country. A universal story of the combat veteran.

Valkyrie

I watch Valkyrie from the backseat of the camouflaged vehicle we're riding in, my knees pressed against a Soviet-era rifle, wooden stock and barrel, that's stuffed into the back of Sergei's seat. Dylan and I ditched our fixer for these last few days on the front line in eastern Ukraine. Even our backup driver is gone at this point. He's picking up a journal I left behind in Avdiivka, another frontline town in the Donbas. I'm on a high, lost in translation with a Russian and a Ukrainian, neither of whom speak English.

There's an understood brotherhood between those who have fought wars.

Dylan's got my equipment on his lap. Valkyrie keeps switching the music; she never lets a song end. She passes a bottle of Stella back to me for another sip. I pass it to Dylan. Earlier, at a gas station restaurant, she ripped her unit's Velcro patch from her shoulder sleeve and stuffed it into her pocket, a blatant and conscious decision that she's going to drink and break the rules tonight.

Sergei, Valkyrie's driver and comrade, keeps singing her real name, "Yuuuuuuliiyaa," half scolding and half in adoration, a "What are you doing now, crazy one?" type of voice, as she switches to yet another song. I laugh and look at Dylan; he turns to me, smiling, because she's wild, angry, full of fire. She hides the beer at her feet as we slow down at another checkpoint to exit Toretsk, the frontline town where her unit is based, the city center home to a war-destroyed, former town hall less than two kilometers from the front line. We drive through, slow down and brake again as we curve around a series of ditches and craters created by the war's mortars and artillery shelling. As we pick up speed again, she jacks the music back up, finds another song on her phone, lights another cigarette, and shakes her long hair loose. The headlights of a car driving in the opposite direction briefly accent the wavy amber of what looks more like the mane of a lion in the night.

I met Valkyrie a few days earlier, during a scheduled interview through my fixer, Dubas, who knew her from the earliest years of the war. They were both *volunteer* soldiers back then, serving in a *volunteer battalion*, a concept completely unfamiliar to me before I first stepped foot inside Ukraine. Where I came from, the term *veteran*, at least in the realm of war and military, equated to one thing only: a civilian who raised their right hand, took the oath to serve and signed a contract to defend their country, then in turn was paid, educated, armed, trained and provided healthcare, and after fulfilling their obligation, suddenly began to give a shit about Veterans Day. But as I would learn, this blanket definition didn't apply to Ukrainian war veterans, especially those who were on the front line in 2014, during the beginning of the war. And it especially didn't apply to Yuliia Tolopa, which was even more of a reason to meet her.

She spoke entirely in Russian during our interview, hunched over on a stool inside an old, abandoned brick warehouse converted into frontline military living quarters, a room with barely enough space for the few tables and five or so military cots that were crammed inside. I sat across from her on the cot offering the most space, closest to the pocket door where earlier I had smacked my head against the frame on the way in, and then, as directed by Valkyrie, using the Sharpie she handed me, I had marked a star at the end of a series of rows of other stars indicating previous whacks of misfortune.

Leaning forward, sharp chin, strong nose, wide mouth and pale-blue wolf eyes made prominent by hair pulled back tightly into a bun, she rested her elbows on her knees, her hands clasped together while listening to Dubas interpret my first question. I could see the tattoo of a feather beginning on the outside of her thumb past the knuckle, wrapping up and around her wrist under a white boldfaced watch and a collection of brightly colored, youthful string bracelets: a green, the blue and yellow of Ukraine's flag, the black and red of the Right Sector nationalist party. A daisy dangled from a black band around her neck, next to a silver Ukrainian crest on a chain.

"What were you doing before Maidan? What was your life like?" I asked what felt like a stupid first question for the interview, but where does one even begin with a story such as Valkyrie's? With a person who I already understood was branded as a Russian traitor, who left her home and her country when she was only eighteen years old, who months later nearly died fighting in a war against it?

It all went back to 2014. To the Euromaidan Revolution in Kyiv. To the revolutionaries continuing their fight in Eastern Ukraine as volunteer soldiers of a new war, fighting for something they believed in, not because a government deployed them or told them it was the right thing to do. It all went back to this brand of patriotism that was so far from my reality of military service.

TORNADO OF PATRIOTISM

I often have to remind myself that not everyone in America shares the understanding of the phrase *9/11* that I and so many others share. That twenty years is enough time to create a generation of men and women who know about it but can't feel an instant, burning visceral memory abyss of replayed scenes. The fire and explosions; the intentional, malicious turn as the passenger jet sliced through the second Twin Tower; the people jumping from windows, their bodies like toy figurines, falling for what felt like an eternity through the blue sky of a perfect September morning. They can't remember the raw terror in voices, the screaming for help, the video reportage of people overseas cheering for the agony and death of American people, the broadcasted executions and decapitations, Daniel Pearl ... the towers crumbling to the ground like sandcastles in the wind. They can't remember the stark understanding that we lived in a world that was capable of this, that we were attacked within our own borders, on our own soil, that this might only be the opening act before nuclear and chemical warfare melted our population to the ground.

They can't remember the fear.

It will remain a day that description, storytelling, and even live footage will never be able to fully justify. Because it wasn't only the horrors of that day; it was the by-product of those events, the reactive energy saturating the air, the sadness, the confusion, the fear, the pride, the hate, the love, the conflicting emotions oozing from our pores and into the air because there just wasn't enough room for them to stay locked within our own beings. And within the space above, they tangled together, trapping us under a dome where we inhaled each other's exhales of recycled emotions, creating a storm that gave wind to a tornado of patriotism.

Anyone alive, present and old enough in the United States would have to remember it. Near Fort Stewart in southeast Georgia, home to plenty of military units, it seemed like *everyone* supported the troops, wove banners and flags. Lines snaked around sidewalks at recruitment stations across the country as thousands waited to enlist in the service. Stripes and stars were everywhere— on posters, t-shirts, pins, ribbons; on "proud mom and dad of a soldier" bumper stickers at every traffic light; on the wrappers of "freedom burgers" and "freedom fries" at fast food joints.

Driving home every day from my job in the Army, back into the civilian world in fatigues, it was like exiting the phone booth as Superman, hearing honks and "thank you for your service" coming from every direction. That Lee Greenwood song "God Bless the U.S.A." played over and over again inside every public and private space with a working sound system. It was the same song I used to innately reject; a reminder of West Point's motivational, patriotic brainwash videos they made us watch after a session of complete demoralization. But the song became something different, and even I found myself cranking up the volume in my car, letting it stir a fire of pride in my gut every time he'd roll into the chorus, a thank you to soldiers who pay the cost of American freedom.

It makes it hard to filter through, to sort through the layers of fear that I know had to have been there; the fear that I wrote about in my journal, the fear of being under attack and the beginning of a potential World War III; the fear of going to war and knowing that if we did, I'd be thrown right into the middle of it.

~

No matter how strong and sharp the mind may be in remembering, a memory is often just a framed picture in time or a piece of visual art, hanging on the wall in a museum for the present-day self to observe and speculate upon years and years later. Without realizing it, ideas can be evoked, often false assumptions of who we were and how we felt as the person inside the frame, based on who we are now, standing on the outside. But no one can be the same person they were years ago; not when we've been molded by space and time and the experience of life. If we want to understand who we were in that moment, to speak our most authentic voice, we have to do more than stand and judge from outside the frame. We have to step inside it by searching for an emotion.

When I look for fear after 9/11, I can find it through one of those memories, sometime in October 2001, when President George W. Bush addressed a nation eager to understand what was next, eager to make the fear and uncertainty go away, hoping to find some way to go back to the way things were, when we felt safe and comfortable in the world. I'm in my apartment in Savannah, just home from work, uniform half on, the time of year when it's too dark too early. Looking through the sliding glass door that leads to my little balcony as I ping back and forth in the hallway, getting ready for the next morning's 0600 briefing followed by PT, I pause and gravitate back to the television, my senses heightened and on alert by a new tone of confidence in his voice.

"Justice," he says. "Faith ... decision ... I ..."

Nausea pinches at the pit of my stomach. I know what's coming, but I don't want it to come, or at least I don't think I do. Yet there's a strange mix of excitement in my gut, a thrill, and as the crowds stand up, clapping with tears in their eyes as he talks about air strikes, the sound unifies into one, loud song, overbearing in the reality of what I signed up for, the reality of what I knew it could mean, the fact that it was becoming a reality.

I was twenty-three years old, signing for a flak jacket. I was twenty-three years old, and I didn't even know what life insurance was. I thought the term next of kin only applied to real adults, or people with children. I was twenty-three years old, being asked by a lady across the table to write down a name, a person to receive the $250,000 from the government if I died in combat, so I wrote down my older brother's name. I was twenty-three years old, and this wasn't a part of the plan. But there really wasn't space to pause and consider the reality of what everything meant. Because ultimately, every feeling was swept away, right into the tornado of 9/11 patriotism.

OLD GRADS

DECEMBER 10, 2016
NEW ORLEANS, LOUISIANA

I recognized Dylan when he walked in that day, into a stuffy, re-served back room of the Ole Saint, a greasy pub in the French Quarter and the selected location for the New Orleans "Old Grad" viewing of the Army-Navy football game. We had been classmates at West Point, although our memories of each other were quite different. He claims we were in the same platoon during Yuk year summer training, Camp Buckner, alleged by some to be even shit-tier than Beast summer training, where an average class of 1,200 might lose more than 200 new cadets over the eight weeks of men-tal and physical beatdowns and bring-you-ups. But I remembered Dylan from the classroom, English 201 to be specific, the only semi-creative class included in West Point's curriculum. I had a vague memory of him standing to read some kind of beautiful, in-tense poem he'd written for homework.

I had no intention of watching the game with them that day. I had no interest in small talking with stiff, retired West Pointer generals and colonels about what I'd been doing with my life since getting out of the Army. I was a freelance photographer, a writer, some kind of artist. No description measured up to the work I had been doing before becoming a civilian, no matter how hard I tried.

Maybe the looming possibility of a fifteenth consecutive loss to Navy encouraged the Association of Graduates regional leaders to scour the earth for those of us who had dropped from the face of it. Because somehow, I was magically added to the New Orle-ans alumni email list after I'd been successfully dodging them and their annual events for years. It might have been perfect timing, because I was also exhausted from trying to round up a popula-tion of LSU fans and top ten NCAA football fans in New Orleans to join me in watching "America's football game" each year. Which led to the culmination point of me sitting there at a table, watching Dylan beeline his way over to me from the entrance, wearing the old school, cadet athlete's letterman sweater that I'd never be caught dead wearing, looking at me as if I would somehow remember his name.

Not that it's common to know a first name at West Point to begin with, but what I learned about Dylan that day was how much he'd accomplished since getting out of the service, and not in a corporate, bullet points for the resume type of career that I would have expected of most West Pointers. He had literally built an entire neighborhood from the ground up in eastern New Orleans, something he titled an "intentional community" for returning veterans of war. But what really got my attention was when he started talking about going back to Iraq for a new project, to a Yazidi village of his former translator that had since been ravaged by ISIS.

"When are we going back to Iraq?" I asked him months later via text, an indirect but direct push at him to solidify his plans; I had every intention to tag along.

"After we go to Ukraine," he said.

"Ukraine? What's in Ukraine?"

"The War in the Donbas with Russia. If you want to go, you need to meet John Boerstler."

John must have sensed my eagerness within minutes of our informal meeting at Grit's Bar in New Orleans, which was rumored to be haunted. That seemed accurate, seeing as how we were the only two customers in the entire joint. The emptiness was a reminder that there should have been three of us, because it was in fact Dylan's meeting, a meeting that I would casually drop in on but wasn't bound to by time or attendance. But then Dylan conveniently called in late, leaving me hesitant to show up at all, my nature to avoid cold meetings with people in the "professional" world without a connection point present. John immediately destroyed my perception.

He was a US Marine combat veteran who finished his service as a Non-Commissioned Officer (NCO), the kind of soldier I felt far more connected to than those of the officer breed, where I errone-ously expected him to come from being leader in the veteran NGO world. He was following up on a fellowship in Ukraine, organizing an international summit in Kyiv to kick-start the country's devel-opment of a ministry of veterans affairs. Since the beginning of the conflict in 2014, he explained, more than 250,000 soldiers had de-ployed to the front line in the Donbas in the war against Russia, only to return to a society without a support system in place.

"So, you want to come?"

Of course I did, but I wasn't sure if John had an accurate per-ception of me. I didn't have any special qualifications like Dylan, to speak on a panel and network with experts in the veteran support industry. In fact, there was nothing professional on my resume since leaving the Army eleven years earlier, nothing to show for it except three years of serious confusion over what I wanted to do with my life, culminating with eight years of an all-over-the-place freelance photography career. But I was more than willing to docu-ment the event for him; it would be an access point into not only a new side project, but something familiar. War. Soldiers. Veterans. Something that this void inside of me had been calling toward ever since leaving the Army. A void that took me over ten years to realize was connected to the same place I had always been counting down the days to escape.

"How do I get to the front line?" I asked, the underlying motive and, ultimately, what placed me on that barstool. War photogra-phy had always seemed like a faraway dream, an inaccessible path without a journalism degree and the natural course of connections that followed. And now here was John, a well-connected supporter of the soldier community and no stranger to Ukraine, holding a door open for me that otherwise I'd have to kick down.

"You want to go to the front? Sure, I can connect you with the right people who can help."

"I'm going with you," Dylan demanded from a third barstool, arriving late to the conversation.

"I'll be your bag boy."

Nearly fourteen years earlier, I had been crossing the border back into Kuwait on our final convoy, thanking a God I wasn't so sure I believed in. And now the thought of going back into a war zone, and not even my own country's war, was putting blood in my veins.

Iryna Tsvila

Translated Excerpt from Interview
Kyiv, Ukraine, 2018

The rights of citizens were violated. Those who have power, and those who are wealthy and their friends, they have their own rules, and for the others there is law. It was a very big distortion to the side of injustice. And when people are indifferent ... then all comfortable conditions are formed for them.

I said, "People, in order to have flowers on the ground, we have to preserve this land first!" If we were a more active society ... we would be able to choose, that is, not let all things happen by themselves and we would live better.

When the Maidan began, I was inspired ... I saw that people were united by the idea of not working only for themselves ... but for the sake of society; they were ready to give something away and to do something.

Kyiv, not Kiev

April 2018
Kyiv, Ukraine

There was some kind of energy in Kyiv. It was something radioactive, charged and connected and at the same time unresolved, but not in a way of losing religion or waving the white flag of surrender. It was more like teetering on an edge, or nearing a point of spontaneous combustion, as if one final unprovoked fissure in the ice would open the abyss to swallow all of us into its depths. I could feel it standing there in the center of Independence Square, the congregation point of the Maidan Revolution. And I could feel it while walking with Alina Viatkina, a cherubic and fiery twenty-two-year-old with the pale, green-blue eyes of a Slav, who in November 2013 was only eighteen, finding her way into the crowd of a small, peaceful protest, a new student at the university in Kyiv, chasing a Twitter feed, following the bandwagon of youth and freedom in protest against not only Ukrainian President Viktor Yanukovych's sudden refusal to sign into the European Union, but against a history of government corruption and civil rights violations that was seeded decades before she was born. Those Slavic eyes—they all seemed to have them—a mixture of gunpowder resin and glacier ice. But it wasn't just a color. There was an intensity behind them—of the past, of the present, of the future, and maybe from before they were born, brandished by a history of starvation and massacres, trial and pain, leaving a past softness frozen behind stone.

Alina gazes into the wind and air in silence as memories come flooding back to her. Not a tear wells up, not even when she shows me the place where her friend Ustym was shot through the head on Instytutska Street, after the government authorized the use of live ammunition to quiet the protesters, and snipers unleashed rounds from the rooftops of Kyiv's ornate parliament buildings.

12

"I can't cry. Still," she says.

We met only hours before she walked me through the sites of the revolution. She was standing on the street curb outside the flat I rented in Kyiv, nervously pulling on a cigarette as my taxi arrived. It was our first planned interview, scheduled within three hours of my landing at Borispol International Airport in Ukraine for the first time. But jet lag wasn't a concern. I was in awe over her story, the bits and pieces I'd already learned. Resting and wasting time wasn't an option.

We were introduced semi-accidentally when I was still back in the US, during a scheduled Skype call with a different volunteer veteran, trying to navigate the origins of the war in Ukraine and who exactly figured into John's 250,000 soldiers deployed and returned since 2014 statistic. If I was going to Ukraine, especially if I was going into the conflict zone, I had to have more than just an unclarified desire to place myself in danger.

Dylan's adamancy to tag along only made me question my motives further. Going to the front line, getting tangled in my photographic adventures, certainly wasn't part of his required itinerary. But was it part of mine? I wasn't on assignment, and clearly this was well beyond the scope of the *New Orleans Advocate* and FEMA. I didn't yet have a clear picture of who or what awaited me in Ukraine beyond a war, soldiers, and veterans.

Further research created even more confusion, the scraps of materials available in English providing a convoluted maze of soldier and veteran demographics, not broken down into Army, Navy, Marines, or Special Forces, but dominated by a recurring term, "volunteer battalion."

Volunteer battalion?

After bogging John down with a bazillion questions to clarify my curiosity, he happily connected me to a direct source of the information, a volunteer veteran of the statistics himself.

"So, we're not like real veterans, not how you are like veteran," Dima Lavrenchuk, call sign "Babay," explained through the computer screen. A vague piece of information that I was already aware of, but that's about all I would extract from him that day;

our meeting coincided with the only free evening he had, one that he was also spending with his "brothers in arms," and by the time I dialed in, it was apparent the celebration had started hours earlier. After plenty of laughs but not enough coherency to answer my detailed list of questions, the crowded Skype screen of war veterans with beverages talking over each other in broken English and Ukrainian broke off and trailed into another room, leaving a lone standing female in front of my screen with her headphones. Alina Viatkina, a war veteran herself. A volunteer paramedic, as she would explain to me.

Even through the computer screen, there was something about her eyes. And now in person, sitting with her in Kyiv, I couldn't stop looking at them.

"You talk too fast," she said matter-of-factly from the other side of the breakfast table, not long after we settled into recording, a reminder of my grandmother nagging over the same thing. But she spoke English in what seemed like a perfect pace, pausing now and then to find a word on Google translator or using a form of charades as she took me through the details of what felt like her first war, a war before the War in the Donbas—the revolution, Maidan, an apocalyptic, urban battleground saturated in a cloud of chemicals and smoke from the fires, grenades and gunfire, right there in the center of the city. In the same place I was watching vendors entertain children with balloons and flying toys, where locals used exotic animals or dressed as giant plush characters to convince passersby and tourists to exchange cash for photo ops. Life went on as if nothing had ever happened there. Life went on as if there wasn't a war still happening six hours away on the express train to Kostyantynivka.

She was still haunted by the sounds of the train. She'd ridden it to the East many times in 2014, although sometimes she'd hitchhike, fundraising medical supplies on Twitter and then delivering them to the hospitals on the front line. Until the day that it wasn't enough, when she decided she had to "be on the war," as she described it. When she decided to be a volunteer paramedic, then found herself dodging the fragments of Grad rockets in country

14

fields and hiding from Russian tanks under a bridge in Pisky, in between evacuating the wounded in a beat-up car, learning how to save lives on the go, and often learning how to reconcile with not saving them.

Volunteer soldiers. The entire concept was something out of fiction before now. That just ordinary men and women, some who had never fired a weapon in their lives, went into a warzone and learned on the fly—by being handed a sniper rifle or becoming tank operators by jumping into an abandoned Infantry Fighting Vehicle in the midst of a firefight. They walked, hitchhiked, rode buses, and took trains to self-deploy of their own free will, to fight for something that came from within, something real. Whether they continued to fight for the ideals of the revolution or to defend their country, their homes, their families, and their friends, they all shared one commonality, the need to contribute and be a part of the cause. To fight in this war that I barely knew a thing about before this, and a war that was still on-going, four years later.

Pitch Black

So this was fear. Or was it adrenaline? Or was it the sound of my heart pounding into my chest, radiating into my ears? Or the sound of the C-17's jets screaming through the air?

I sat there in blackness, strapped to the sidewall in the belly of the aircraft, my stomach twisting at the thought of breaking a promise to call my mom before boarding the last leg of our journey.

A red light briefly illuminated the area in flashes, indicating ten minutes before landing, and within the red bursts and moving bars of shadows I could finally see the others scattered among the cargo, among the shipping containers, the Humvee, the dozer chained to the floor in front of me. A seamless expression threaded across their faces as we loaded our magazines with ammunition: this was real.

There were no windows to catch a snapshot of the world on the other side of the metal, and there was no one to help us visualize; no soldier had walked down this path and returned to tell a story. Our only expectations manifested from untamed imagination and the understanding that we were entering a territory where others wanted us as dead as those in the towers on 9/11.

The red light flickered off, trailing into absolute darkness, a blackout tunnel before the first drop on a thrill-seeking roller coaster ride. There was nothing to see now, only to feel, adrenaline and cortisol running amok, my stomach entering Olympic-caliber gymnastics as it counteracted the sudden movements of the C-17— the surges, drops, dives, and turns.

Nausea.

Before takeoff in Diego Garcia, the Air Force pilots briefed us on a tactical landing in Kandahar: random, chaotic movements on descent to thwart a potential enemy attack from the mountains. We'd fly at night, and thirty minutes before landing, they'd shut down all possible illumination, putting the vessel into blackout mode to camouflage us in darkness. The only light we'd see for the duration of the flight would be the brief flashing of the red light: ten minutes to landing, load your weapons.

Another drop ... this one too long, way too long.

Were we going down? Or was this the tactical landing?

How could it be that I was sitting there, wondering if our bird would take shots from enemy fire in the mountains, and my friends and family were possibly out on the town or deliberating over a movie rental? Or better yet, that they were reading the story of my life in the newspaper instead of hearing it from my mouth?

How could it be, the reality of these simultaneous events unraveling so independently of one another? That while I might come face to face with death, they would be turning out the lights to go to sleep, and they wouldn't have any idea until the dreaded knock on the door?

I exhaled a breath of anxiety as the wheels of the C-17 brushed, bounced, and then rolled against something solid outside. My head, top-heavy from my helmet, orchestrated one last rock of the body, back and forth, to the final halt of the plane.

The sound of the jets revving died down in a slow whistle, eventually giving way to silence, and I began to hear the nervous shuffling of our small body movements as we sat there waiting.

An isolated ping outside set off a melody of metallic clinks, clanks and then a mechanical whirring as the back hatch of the C-17 cracked open, its jaw dropping slowly like the mouth of a prehistoric whale getting ready to regurgitate us into the abyss.

At first, there was no contrast between the sky outside and the blackness within, but once the hatch touched the ground and my eyes finally adjusted, I understood the true definition of pitch black: stars illuminating like a billion fiery suns burning holes through a canopy of ink.

As we walked to the edge of the ramp, I desperately dug into my rucksack for a pair of gloves. They said Afghanistan was harsh in the winter, but I hadn't believed it until a gust of bitter wind bore into my hands like smoldering pins of fiberglass and ice.

A single glowing red light appeared, floating in the air at the bottom of the ramp; we walked down in a single file line, loaded down with our gear slung across our backs, our weapons braced in the ready position, and silently followed a faceless guide down the runway and into the blackness.

Dmytro "Da Vinci" Kotsiubailo

Translated Excerpt from Interview
Avdiivka, Ukraine, 2018

The war is going on; people suffer and are killed every day. No matter how hard it is, somehow we have to finish this thing. The guys that were fighting believed in victory and they wouldn't want us, the last volunteers, to just leave everything like this.

APRICOT TREES

"Do you remember how random Iraq was?" Dylan blurted into the darkness. The roadside bombs, the mortar attacks, death. His words came right as I'd finally conquered my own anxieties about the decision we'd made hours earlier. It was a scene reminiscent of lights-out at summer camp, the kid who wouldn't shut up, or who would stop talking only long enough for you to reach the threshold of spinning into sleep before snapping you back into vivid consciousness with some meaningless thought, just to ensure they weren't the only ones still awake. Except this certainly wasn't camp, and Dylan's silence for the preceding five minutes—and the entire evening—for that matter, made it easy to believe in his confidence, the alibi I needed to convince myself that this was a necessary move as a photojournalist. It was an alibi to believe that we weren't just two American combat veterans falling short of an adrenaline addiction, lured to relive some feeling of danger.

"Fuck you, Dylan! Are we being stupid?"

Silence again as we both stared wide-eyed at the ceiling, lying on our backs on two cot-sized beds squished entirely too close to each other.

"We'll be fine."

We were holed up in a hotel room in Kostyantynivka, the arrival and departure point for most of the frontline towns in the Donetsk region of eastern Ukraine. Our fixer, Dubas, had taken us for a late dinner at his own choice of restaurants nearby, a randomly upscale and conveniently expensive establishment with an oligarch VIP vibe. Per the fixer's terms, lodging and meals went on our tab, along with fuel for the road and a full tank upon his departure... and an apparent fill-up of the empty tank he arrived with early that morning, after he picked us up from our rental flat in Kyiv for the long haul into eastern Ukraine.

"Dude, Jenn. We're in Ukraine," Dylan had said from the back seat of Dubas's jeep as we drove on the M-03, the main latitudinal highway connecting the far west Carpathian Mountains to the eastern industrial Donbas, which before the conflict had continued on into Russia. Instead of the ten-hour (on a good day) drive from Kyiv to Kostyantynivka, Dubas recommended more than once that we take the train instead, to save four hours of travel time and his tires from the road. What began as a relatively well-maintained highway gradually evaporated with each hour separating us from Kyiv, then took a final plunge after passing through Kharkiv. Concrete crumbled into a warped passage of rock, tar and dirt weaving through swaths of meteoric-like fissures, ravines and holes wide enough to swallow half a vehicle.

"You don't understand, the roads ..."

Truth. But I didn't care to understand. I wanted to drive. To roll down the windows and breathe the air, to feel the wind on my skin, to take in the landscape of this new world that had felt so disconnected and foreign until now. On a map, yes, one could see the borders of Europe, that traveling to Amsterdam or Sweden was a simple three-hour flight from Kyiv. But the EU felt light years away. Ukraine was removed, undiscovered and uncharted, a faraway land with a war on its borders.

Even Kyiv carried an apprehension of the unknown before I'd walked the streets and breathed its air, the nights leading to my departure from New Orleans overwhelmed with returning dreams of the C-17 or being back on some dream-warped version of a battlefield in Iraq. But now that I was there, and now that we were heading east into the deeper unknown, closer to the border of the war, there was this new exhilaration in being so disconnected from the other side, from my world at home that was still left in a state to only imagine.

"Do you want to go?" the English-speaking soldier asked us minutes before we departed to the restaurant in Kostyantynikva with Dubas that evening, coordinating over a handheld radio, the beep of his last transmission still echoing through an empty hallway covered with taped-up blue and yellow "dear soldier" drawings from Ukrainian children. We were only two kilometers from the frontline positions near Avdiivka, standing on the third floor of a characterless Soviet-era concrete flat building converted into an operations center for the Right Sector volunteer soldiers.

"Please understand. It's very, very dangerous."

Not even a moment of hesitation, at least not verbally. But his words continued to swarm through my head like wasps, bashing against my skull until they finally knocked themselves unconscious for a second time after Dylan's interruption, allowing me to fall into some sort of sleep.

~

It was a perfect morning for photography, when the clouds and sun are positioned in such a way that the eyes cannot stop attaching and attracting the lens, when everything takes on a new dimension of life. When even a village weathered by industry and war carries a beauty created in contrast. Dense white clouds of apricot tree petals giving life to the monotonous, gray, flat buildings towering like tombstones around the glaring, golden rooftops of Orthodox churches. Narrow roads vanishing into tunnels of bright green, the trees seeming to entirely encircle us before spitting us out into the next landscape, where abandoned, brick factories crumbled in time before the unearthly mountain ranges of coal mining deposits.

Hand on the camera's shutter, I was itching to capture it all. But drive-by, out-of-focus photography through a car window was the only option once we left the Route 66 gas station at the edge of Toretsk, the meeting point for this trip to the frontline positions near the occupied city of Horlivka with Da Vinci, the Right Sector volunteer soldier I had interviewed the previous day in Avdiivka.

"Don't take photos of the tanks," he warned as we turned away from the concrete onto a hidden dirt road, brushing against tree branches that pushed through the windows as we passed tanks dug deep into the ground. And then the forest gave way to an open space without a road, our car rocking side to side like a small fishing boat on tropical-storm-caliber swells as we slowly ascended and descended across a muddy, raw terrain, eventually finding our way back onto a residential road.

A front line running right through a neighborhood that some clearly still called home. Old men and women walked and rode bicycles past military vehicles, pulling wagons of produce around craters left by mines and mortars, passing weathered blue-, red- and green-painted entry gates perforated with bullet holes and stucco exteriors decorated in shrapnel scars. It was like a functioning ghost town, the few remaining locals carrying on with their lives, moving around, past and through the soldiers who repurposed abandoned homes and shops into living quarters, kitchens and medical stations. And only twenty meters away, trenches like those in World War I zigged and zagged deep throughout the earth.

Nothing was what I imagined. Including the entire volunteer movement, people still volunteering on the front line of the conflict four years later and well after the government reestablished control. No government escorts were required to reach them. Even over the last few days, there was barely a slowdown to check press credentials as Dubas flew through the multiple checkpoints layered throughout the ATO (Anti-Terrorist Operation), swerving around the concrete slowdown barriers as Dylan and I smashed against the side walls in the hollowed-out back space of a WWII-era ambulance van he had swapped out for his jeep in Kostyantynikva.

The Ukrainian Volunteer Corps of the Right Sector, one of the last, if not the last, of the volunteer battalions still left to be integrated under the Ministry of Defense, or the government, ran its own operation on the front line. And they weren't begging to be integrated. They preferred to remain unofficial and "illegal," as their status on paper and under the law declared. That's really all it was, a piece of paper, because, in reality, the message was casually ignored. The State needed them right where they were, working alongside and mixed in with the soldiers of an understaffed Army that couldn't defend the front line alone. So why not join the Army at this point? Not only were the Right Sector volunteers ineligible for the standard soldier and veteran benefits, but their lives didn't even enter the statistics of KIAs on the front line. But did it even matter? Because those who did enter the statistics often became faceless spec and dump numbers collected by a disconnected world for reports and skimmed-over news headlines.

"They don't do anything for us. Why should I ask anything of them?" Da Vinci had answered during his interview, when I asked why he or the others didn't want to integrate into the official Army. He was only eighteen, an art student in Lviv, when he ran to Maidan and then to conflict. Now a hardened twenty-two-year-old commander of his company, he had shrapnel-scarred and weathered skin, the spirit of a painter seemed all but lost under his black eyes.

He, like many, had no trust in the government, in the Army. No trust in the leadership. Lingering tales of corrupt former Soviet generals working for the other side during the height of the war, giving life to the system of bribery that plagued Soviet times and still managed to plague Ukraine in its years of "independence." The kind of bribes that fattened a few men's wallets in turn for the lives of possibly thousands in 2014 and 2015.

"The enemy is there; they can see us," Da Vinci said, pointing to the top of a refuse hill only five hundred meters in the distance. And less than a meter from one of Da Vinci's bunkers, Dylan stood in a crater left by an artillery round that had landed only a few days earlier. You could still smell the gunpowder.

"Can you ask these guys why they fight?" Dylan asked Dubas, a question for the huddle of soldiers smoking nearby. Because it was clear that they were sitting targets, and they weren't ignorant of that fact. The enemy knew exactly where they were. Drone footage over the years gave a clear map of the positions they were locked to remain in and defend by the so-called peace agreements. Peace agreements that only prevented a full-scale, politically declared attack across the entire 400-kilometer chunk of eastern Ukraine that was already sectioned off, dividing families, friends and worlds that once spent a lifetime together. Every day, every night was a roll of the dice, a testing of grounds, a matter of mood, to squeeze the trigger or to not squeeze the trigger.

"For my country. To protect the borders," Dubas answered for the first soldier.

"He can't be more than eighteen years old," Dylan whispered as we walked away. "What is he doing here?"

But part of it made sense to me. Standing there with them in this place, I felt more at peace than I'd felt in years. It was something about the simplicity of being back in that disconnected, parallel universe we jumped into when first landing in Afghanistan. The universe where we continued to move forward while our world at home moved forward on its own. It didn't matter that this wasn't Afghanistan or Iraq or that I wasn't with the same people. Because in essence, I was with the same people. I was in the same place. There was something timeless and connected here.

SNAPSHOTS

I AM A PHOTOGRAPHER. Some might call me a documentary photographer, others a photojournalist. I don't have a degree in journalism or photography or multimedia arts. I don't take cover photos for *National Geographic* or *The New York Times*. And I don't own or understand all the different models of professional cameras, lenses, high-tech accessories, and studio equipment.

For me, a photograph that carries meaning is a moment captured. Growing up, it was a memory before anything else. I always had a disposable camera in hand, probably an effort to preserve the moments of my life that I wanted not only to remember but to preserve—places abruptly pushed out of reach because we moved so many times over the years, friendships broken short as we went our different ways in life. Those moments sit in stacks of scrapbooks in my storage unit, melded onto pages that have yellowed over the decades, right next to ziplock bags filled with handwritten letters scribbled over a decade of maturing penmanship. *B.F.F. I miss you. When are you coming to visit? Stay safe. We're so proud of you. Come home.*

Digital photography and cell phones weren't exactly accessible back then, or they certainly weren't on the personal packing list to stuff away in a footlocker or a rucksack bound for Afghanistan in late 2001 and early 2002. We mailed letters, and on mail day, if we were lucky, we received letters, sometimes packed inside boxes loaded with candy, cigarettes, ramen noodles, movies to play on portable DVD players, and extra rolls of camera film or disposable cameras.

The last bulk of handwritten letters I received, before the digital black hole era swallowed tangible media, were addressed to me at the APO mailbox in Kandahar. When I wrote back, at least to my family, my words were often ambiguous, a translated version comprehensible to the world I left behind. *It's hot ... it's dusty and dirty ... I was an idiot for bringing my contact lenses ... we haven't had showers for three weeks ... my platoon is building the guard tower for the Taliban detainee facility on base ... don't worry.* Nothing that I wrote about in my journal, nothing about fear or wondering if I'd be alive the next morning, nothing about feeling a loss of why we were there.

Instead, I sent them my rolls of film and disposable cameras to be developed. It was easier for me to communicate my new world visually, through snapshots of my life as I was living it, without thought or interpretation attached. Just snapshots of the moments I wanted to preserve and remember, images that years later would help me remember and see history through a new pair of eyes. But ultimately, in the moment of taking them, these snapshots helped me stay in the moment instead of counting down the days, to focus on the world surrounding us and the natural wonders and beauty of life. Because even in war, those are the things that remain consistent and present, as long as our eyes are open to see them.

THE ROOM

I have a picture of the room where I woke up that first morning in Kandahar. One side is blurred by the pink orb of my finger covering part of the lens, but it's clear the focus is on an archway that led from my room into the hallway of the building. A camouflage tarp hangs from above it for privacy, and from within the room, it looks like there used to be a molding or a door frame that was ripped away, leaving this raw, exposed, disorderly path of internal wall, at least eight inches wide, skirting the entire perimeter of the opening.

At a glance, you'd probably only see the rawness of it, the exposed section of the wall, or this makeshift tarp door hanging over a giant, blown-out hole in a wall. For years, that's all I would remember—a blown-out hole in the wall, not an archway or a doorway. I'd only remember what fascinated me enough to take the photograph in the first place: the rawness of the situation or the unknowns of this deeply turbulent past that lingered all around us. I'd only remember the scar, and that the scar was a product of violence and war.

A blown-out hole in the wall, a doorway that probably used to have a door that a soldier or a team of soldiers kicked in, trying to capture an enemy on the other side, ripping the hinges and frame right out of the wall as they came barreling through. Or maybe a soldier blew it open with a hand grenade, or a team of them blasted through it with thousands of AK-47 rounds. Maybe it happened when the Soviets took over, or maybe it happened only a few weeks prior, when the Taliban made their last stand against the Northern Alliance.

I have a second picture from the same camera, taken almost immediately after. This one focuses on a cot, one of the two that

28

were inside. It's pushed up against the left wall, and my gear is strewn all over it and under it: my boots, rucksack, duffle bag and everything I blindly unloaded in the dark the night before; my desert field jacket, gas mask, Kevlar, M16, canteens and that stupid tactical flashlight that didn't work worth a damn to navigate through the pitch black. But next to the cot, there are two random chairs, just lingering awkwardly in the middle, taking up space.

They weren't the kind of chairs we would have brought with us, the standard metal foldouts; these were much nicer, with armrests and cushions, like real furniture that was there before us, furniture that belonged to the room. But then…who did the room belong to? Because it felt like they were still there, like I was inhaling the same air they'd exhaled only moments before, or that some kind of activity was just taking place, and then in mid-action, they'd just abandoned ship, vanished into thin air.

I imagine how many lives must have passed through the room over the decades of war, and how many different soldiers could have sat in one of those two chairs that were left behind, writing letters home. Were they fighting because they had to? Were they scared? Were any of them really any different from me?

Whenever I remember Kandahar, I always think of the chairs, and it's always from the outside looking in first, as if I'm watching a movie set from above, this overexposed, bright scene of natural light, and the air is the kind of quiet and still that brings on a white noise, except behind the white noise there's real life happening, the faint clinking, harmonic cadence of tent stakes being hammered into the ground outside. I'm sitting on the cot on the right side of the room, and about three feet away, facing toward me, is one of the empty chairs.

The scene changes, and suddenly I'm looking through my own eyes, sitting right across from it. At first, it's empty, but then a boy is sitting there, a soldier from another country, about the same age I was back then, wearing a tan uniform with ribbons and awards pinned above both of his breast pockets. He's calm, sitting up straight and tall, soldier posture, feet flat on the ground, his hands resting gently on an older rifle with a wooden stock and barrel that's laid across his lap. He's looking at me silently, almost as if he's studying me, and his eyes are friendly and peaceful, but they're also sad, with an empty kind of melancholy looming behind them, almost as if he knows he's dead.

Eventually, I'm outside of myself looking in again, and as I watch us sitting there in silence, this boy and I gazing at each other from three feet away, he slowly begins to vanish, evaporating into the air of the room.

VOLODYMYR HALASHCHUK

TRANSLATED EXCERPT FROM INTERVIEW
KYIV, UKRAINE, 2019

And if you know the nature of that heroism, somebody goes to pull a tank out of fire but in reality he was just so drunk that he didn't understand it was burning. But then again, when we were starting the counterattack, we climbed the hill. They were hitting us with everything, even the anti-tank missiles. But I was standing there, my brother beside me. Missiles whizzing about, flying tin and metal. I looked to see who was with me, who was standing there. Time froze, it was like a film, I was seeing everything in slow motion. And it was surprising. The people you would least expect to be there, they were standing there, strongly fighting back.

THE NATURE OF HEROISM

"I don't understand why they lied to his family," Bizhan said, his tone taking a grim turn from the energetic cadence of the interview's previous two hours. Bizhan, like Valkyrie, like Babay, was another of the 2014 Aidar Volunteer Battalion veterans I was becoming quickly acquainted with, right down to integrating the Star Trek Vulcan salute of Bizhan and Babay's self-proclaimed Bob Marley squad into my own routine. Originally from Tajikistan, Bizhan was one of the few, if not the only, volunteer soldiers I'd met who didn't go by a war name or a call sign. He didn't need one. His name, just like his personality, was impossible to confuse with another's, even in the way he spoke English, how his *t*'s, such as in "the," were pronounced as *z*'s.

In the portrait I made of him a few weeks after his interview, Bizhan is wearing someone else's fatigues, a reality of the volunteer movement, wearing whatever country's military attire one could get their hands on. He looks almost regal with his Tajik nose, gazing toward the camera in a stoic pose that for all who knew him could mean he was on the verge of crumbling into either a giggle or a random, philosophical thought designed for an engaged discussion. Instead of holding a rifle to his chest, he's cradling a guitar, and all of this epitomizes him. He doesn't identify himself as a writer, even though he's writing a book. To him, the writing doesn't matter unless it's published or widely known. And he doesn't identify as a musician, although it's clear that if he chose to pursue a path of rock stardom, he'd travel far. Bizhan identifies himself as a biologist or possibly a chemist ... what I would call a blend of mad scientist and conspiracy theorist, forever crazed and chasing new inventions, even if they've already been done. Because Bizhan's idea, as he will tell you, is entirely different ... possibly in a way that only he understands.

The days and weeks throughout that autumn were packed with interviews in Kyiv, the locations rotating throughout the multiple Airbnb flats I rented around the center, moving in and out in between visits to the front line for interviews and constant, last-minute flight changes to prolong my stay into a seeming eternity. I was never ready to go home. But no matter the changing locations, my flat carried with it a growing community of 2014 volunteers, primarily amongst the Aidar veterans, some who hadn't seen each other in years while walking their different directions on the front line or in the peace life. My flat became a centrifugal force, pulling them back together, the evenings following a long day of interviews often transpiring into sleepless nights of comradery and drinking, closing with Babay or Bizhan playing music and leading a drunken choir throughout the night.

Bizhan would often drown himself in the bottle of Cognac he'd arrived with before losing himself in a slouch on the floor in a hypnotic frenzy of musical connectedness, spit flying as he flooded the air with vocal inflections that carried you to some faraway place and time, his whispers traversing into thunderous vibrations as he slammed the untrimmed nylon restrings of his well-worn guitar to the rhythm of a song rooted in Ukrainian folklore. A song of the Cossacks, of legendary fighters, a song that any soldier, without translation, would recognize as one that spoke to the power of revolution.

His interview matched the musician in him, his loud, intermittent laughs forcing a constant adjustment of audio levels, to record quality sound and avoid hearing loss. Every sentence he spoke was armed with animated intensity and preceded by silent, pensive thought as he painted a "kids with guns" version of his journey to the front line in 2014, riding to Starobilsk on a bus with his "hipster" friends, extreme nationalists and simple farmers who casually discussed the prices of cows on their way to the war.

"We just rented a bus, and we go zer. You know, we thought that zis battalion is some regular unit. We just join it and start fighting.

But when we went, we realized it's absolutely self-proclaimed. It was not the military unit! It was like ... zee gang of patriots! Imagine we are standing in zee yard of zee old factory; it was like zee base of zis battalion. And one of the officers is asking, 'Who is not eighteen years old yet? Who was to zee prison?' The third question was 'Who of you have no experience of military service at all?' Yeah and all zose forty people raised their hands ..."

His charisma and deflection of the dark even carried through his story of the day Ruslan, one of his Aidar comrades, was killed in an artillery attack. Bizhan saw his head lifted from his body in the distance and joked over the absurdity of being rushed in as a paramedic, as if there was something he could do with a headless body. But then something happened toward the end, the confidence in his voice fizzling into a kind of uncertainty in what he was trying to convey.

"Someone had told his family that he was killed heroically, covering the whole company when we were retreating. Some fantastic story. Silly thing because he had a normal death in the attack. But you know, it was in fact heroic ... he was killed in an attack, and that's okay."

~

Sometime during the summer of 2003, news of roadside bombs and small arms attacks began trickling into our daily leaders' meeting in Iraq, coming down through the channels of the military hierarchy to our battalion commander, and then pushed forward to our disconnected world where media didn't exist.

One afternoon, after the next day's missions were tasked, logistics addressed, sensitive items accounted for and dreams of ice and air conditioners arriving crushed, the battalion commander closed with his final notes and updates on the latest intelligence dropped into his top-secret email account. He sat at the head of our table in the over 120°F tent, the whirring of our useless "swamp cooler" fan muffled his already exhausted voice as he began to speak. Wiping the sweat and sand from his brow, he began to tell the story of a recent death of a US soldier on the battlefield, his voice barely holding between his intermittent pauses to maintain composure.

I cannot remember anything more about this soldier except that he was a sergeant first class. I can't remember his name because I didn't know him, and he wasn't in our unit. Possibly he was from our infantry division at Fort Stewart, and maybe that's why this story was told among the stories of the hundreds of others who died that year. But what I can remember clearly is the image, what I imagined when the commander told the story. What he described when his voice was shaking, when he tried disguising the tears as drops of sweat to wipe away. This image of a soldier dying under fire in an intense battle, holding back a mass of the enemy single-handedly, throwing himself alone into the fight to save his soldiers. Like something out of a film, I can still see the fire, this blaze of glory, the clean gunshot wound the military reports would summarize as his cause of death. A heroic death.

THE WAR MUSEUM

I HAVE ANOTHER PHOTOGRAPH FROM KANDAHAR, taken around my first week on the ground. It's of eight soldiers from my platoon, and they're in a completely desolate area where everything is the color of sand, from their desert fatigues to the ground they're walking on to the thin strip of blue sky that's screened over with a blanket of sand saturating the air. In the background, there's one of our sand-colored trucks parked to the side. Next to it, though much further in the background, there's a glaring, white-painted wing from what looks like a commercial airliner extending vertically toward the sky, like a corpse reaching out of its grave. It's like a scene out of an apocalyptic movie, the end of time when we've all killed each other and the people in the photograph are the only survivors, trying to put the pieces back together.

This was the war museum.

It's what I called Afghanistan back then, in my journal, in my letters sent home, because it was the only way I could describe what it felt like to wake up in a landscape littered by decades of conflict. It's as if we were walking through one giant exhibit consolidating hundreds of years of war without resolution. As if all the ghosts were still there, walking through the hallways of the war-scarred buildings we occupied or hovering around the wreckage that remained.

I knew nothing of Afghanistan's history before we hit the ground. At least, I didn't know enough. My version of knowledge was glossed over with the current situation: 9/11, Osama bin Laden, terrorism, the Taliban, al-Qaeda, and then in between, a youthful memory of Billy Joel's flash reference to "Russians in Afghanistan" in his 1980s hit song, "We Didn't Start the Fire."

I learned some things on the go, from the seasoned NCOs who had been in the Army long enough to remember the wars of the '80s and '90s. That there was a time when women walked the streets of Kabul, wearing the latest fashions of the West. Or that the United States built the Kandahar airfield decades earlier. Or that the hosts of the welcome feast we were forced to attend, the warlords we had to make nice with, weren't anything close to being the "good guys" I imagined the American Army would partner with, but a necessary evil to befriend in order to carry out the mission.

I remember the war souvenirs. How I had to have them—and strangely, even in the moment of want, I questioned why I wanted these things. Maybe it was a way of normalizing the situation, normalizing the war and the previous wars of a land I walked over without enough understanding.

The local Afghans who worked on the base sold Northern Alliance hats, burkas, and sometimes artifacts from the war museum, probably picked from the fields of debris and unexploded ordinance. Discarded 120mm artillery shells, Kevlar helmets, bayonets. I bought a few of the hats, a bright turquoise burka, and then three of the bayonets for five dollars each. The locals advertised them as "Russian" bayonets, from when the Russians were in Afghanistan, and one of them was customized by the warrior who used it with a special rubber grip wrapped around the handle.

Every time I looked at this bayonet, when I pulled it from storage in the numerous moves I made over the years, I imagined what might have happened to this soldier. I contemplated the sharpness of the blade, the gripping, and the reality that he actually used this bayonet in battle. That he not only affixed it to his rifle but he also held it in his hand in what must have been violent, close-quarter combat, face-to-face slicing and stabbing and blood, not shooting some faceless enemy in the distance.

In my mind, a bayonet was not something of modern warfare. It was simply a decorative addition, a dull blade affixed to an outdated and heavy M14 for drill and ceremony at West Point, until I bought this "Russian" bayonet. Then it became something entirely different, painted with a history of a real human. But even in all this contemplation, in all my imaginings, its history was always attached to a Russian soldier. Not a Soviet soldier, even though I knew it was from the Soviet times. I still equated Soviet to Russian.

"The Soviet Union system was based on the 'divide and conquer' principle," Edward "Edvas" Hatmullin told me almost two decades after I had been in Afghanistan. "I was twenty years old then. We were sent over. It was conscription service; it was not a contract. We were all drafted for compulsory service. We were brought in on a peacekeeping mission, but in reality, it was a war. They just set one against the other and that's all. And at the time we stupidly believed what was being said on TV, and now we actually use our own heads to think."

Edvas was the first volunteer I interviewed in eastern Ukraine, in Kostyantynivka, where he ran a logistics operation out of a storage yard packed with donations from around the world that would supply the entire front line in the Donetsk region. He literally embodied the image of a "steely-eyed killer," but the war spirit all but melted away once a Donbas kitten brushed against his leg and purred its way into his giant palms. It was clear that his wife and children had the same effect on him.

His interview was mostly a surface scrape as I tried to push through his aversion to being the subject of an oral history recording, disguised under half-joking (if not entirely serious) offers to send me home with a live antitank mine in my suitcase. But what I did take away from that day was one critical fact: Edvas had been a soldier in the Soviet Army years before he became involved in the Donbas conflict. And it's this understanding that made me see things about Afghanistan so much more clearly. I began piecing it together in a more connected way. I began to understand how closely connected all wars really are, how none of them truly stand alone. They have always been part of a universal blanket, woven throughout centuries and generations.

The bayonets weren't Russian bayonets, although one of them could have belonged to a Russian soldier, in the same way it could have belonged to a Georgian soldier, a Lithuanian soldier, an Estonian soldier, a Ukrainian soldier who had been conscripted into the Soviet Army and sent into Afghanistan on a "peace-keeping" mission, blindly obeying the orders of a government that he may have believed valued his life and his service. A government he trusted, that rewarded his actions of killing and dying as an act of heroism. A soldier who might have realized, once he hit the ground, that there was nothing peaceful, no honor felt in his actions or the actions he witnessed, that his purpose became simply trying to stay alive long enough to make it back home. A soldier who may have been shipped back to Ukraine, to his family, in a zinc coffin accompanied by some heroic story of his death and a couple new medals to pin on a uniform that he'd never wear again. He may have been a soldier who realized that he was just a pawn in a game he would never understand. A soldier who was just as human as I was when I walked across the same land that he had walked two decades earlier.

DARTH VADER

"Dah-da-da-da, dan-da-da, dan-da-da." An inharmonious version of the foreboding Darth Vader theme echoes through the November night as Valkyrie, Babay, and I sing together boisterously, marching down the slope of a Kyiv street to a corner pub on Maidan Square. There's electricity in the air. You can feel a charge in the words spoken among them and the other veterans walking in the streets, the voltage peaking in their brief exchanges with the huddles smoking outside of Veterano Pizza, Kyiv's central hangout for the 2014 volunteers, as we walk by.

Hours earlier I watched Valkyrie and Babay as they sat entranced at a small breakfast table in my flat, replaying the same video on their phones, broadcast again and again throughout multiple Ukrainian media outlets, of a Russian naval ship attacking a Ukrainian naval ship in the Sea of Azov. Then silence fell as they sat wide-eyed, Valkyrie biting her nails, Babay leaning over her shoulder, both watching the live video she pulled up on her phone, of President Petro Poroshenko addressing the nation.

"He's declared martial law," Babay translates for me, sensing my eagerness to understand what the hell is going on.

Martial law, a term I was mostly familiar with through US Civil War films and the mandated military history courses at West Point. In other words, a law of the past, relevant to American war history, when we fought on our own land. But martial law wasn't part of the archives in Ukraine. For a territory facing centuries of aggression and shifting borders while struggling to maintain some sort of independence, it was as relevant now as it was back then. Strangely, not even in 2014 had it been put into action, not after the illegal annexation of Crimea, not after the Russians infiltrated eastern

Ukraine, when the population fell into a void of incomprehension as they watched their military, stalled in a Soviet mentality of internal policing rather than defending external borders, do essentially nothing in response. In fact, the war in the Donbas wasn't officially considered a war. It was a "conflict," or rather, the "Anti-Terrorist Operation," as the acting president (for the exiled Yanukovych) had named it while simultaneously urging citizens to rise and defend the country. This was the first time since Ukraine's independence from the Soviet Union that the country had declared martial law, an official state of war preparations. And it changed everything.

Valkyrie is amped up. She's heading back to the Donbas on a night train, making phone calls left and right on the way to the station, calling her comrades on the front line for status updates, coordinating a safety plan for her daughter to be moved from the eastern town where a family cares for her to a safer location farther from the front. Because war is in the air. A declaration could go down at any moment, something they've all been waiting for. And she's ready to fight, to end it, to die, to live. Anything would make her happy, as long as it was something different from the never-ending game of waiting. And this *was* different, a change in the monotony of the seemingly never-ending, World War I-type trench warfare the soldiers had been locked into since the peace agreements. Peace agreements that were about as official as the war's official title as a conflict. This was their time. They could finally fight back, take action, avenge their comrades' deaths, and find some kind of closure to move on to the peace life.

The peace life. It was an unfamiliar term when I first stepped foot inside Ukraine, but I became quickly acquainted through its repetition in the numerous oral histories I'd collected throughout Kyiv and on the front line with the volunteers.

It was their equivalent to our civilian world. That place on the other side, a world of normalcy where one could disconnect from war and move on, or where you assumed this would happen. Where you were free to finally live without constraints, to pursue those dreams and ambitions you had before war consumed everything.

"What do you do to heal?" I remembered asking Valkyrie, days after our first interview, returning a text message from a flat in Kyiv.

Anxiety kept her awake that night, no doubt exacerbated by the interview, reliving the stories I pulled from her mind to the forefront of memory, words now running free in the air. Like the day her vehicle detonated a roadside mine en route to a mission, when she came to in a sunflower field.

What I saw is still in front of my eyes. Two bodies torn apart, or rather what was left of those bodies. The smell was monstrous: smoke mixed with TNT with some weird sour smell, with blood, engine oil and earth. The only things I remember from lying on the ground are the blue skies, the sunflowers covered in blood and oil, and silence.

"Drink. Fight. Fuck it … live on," she replied to my question, the unexpected words popping up in Google translator after I cut and pasted the Cyrillic letters of her reply.

Another text followed, "I think I know what this is: PTSD."

I drew a blank, unsure of how to respond. How could a soldier in her situation even begin to process the impact of their experience in war when there was no escaping the proximity of war? When we Americans deployed to Iraq or Afghanistan, we wouldn't have the capacity to understand the mental and physical distresses of war, at least on a conscious level, until returning home—and for many veterans, not until years later. When the rotation was complete, we had the advantage of being completely removed from the land where we had fought. We boarded a C-17, a C-5 or a contracted 747 commercial airliner and flew far away, over the oceans and thousands of miles away, to a land where we could at least physically separate ourselves from the conflict zone. But for Ukraine's soldiers and veterans, the war was perpetually inescapable. A train fare, a car ride, or sometimes only a few kilometers separated the front line from the peace life.

Alina Viatkina was the first to speak of it during her interview: "We went to Pisky, and when we came to this front line I saw the light under Donetsk. It was in the evening and I just saw the light and I asked, 'What is it?' And my driver joked that it was from the shelling. But then I understood. There is a peace life and there is a front line," she had said.

It was apparent that even she had to recalibrate a life's memory, to understand that there was now a front line in the same land where she walked in the peace life, that the two worlds were layered and intertwined in such a way that made a pizza delivery possible across the divide, and a divide that was quite ambiguous and shifting in 2014 and 2015.

Even the notion of a true peace life in Ukraine seemed like a farfetched idea when I arrived, that there could be such a disconnect between realities in a country at war. It seemed to me that as long as war waged on, the entire population would be affected. But I soon realized that didn't matter. There was still an absolute separation of worlds, one home to those who lived only in the conflict and its resolution, and the other home to those completely detached from it.

In interviews it resurfaced again and again. That even during the Maidan, the war before the war, in the middle of the shootings, the water cannons, the chemical grenades and the beatings, that just around the corner people casually went on with their lives, drinking coffee and beer in cafes within earshot of students bleeding out onto the sidewalks and cobblestone streets. People went about their business as if nothing was happening fewer than twenty meters away. Life went on, and the war went on in the same fashion after martial law—which expired after thirty days.

There was never a war declaration. Nothing changed except for new accusations of Poroshenko's move being a last-minute attempt to boost his ratings for the upcoming elections, or to stall elections and remain in power. And Valkyrie is sick of this shit.

It isn't the same war she fought in 2014. She isn't fighting alongside the same comrades, either. She's now under a contract in the Ukrainian Armed Forces with plenty of soldiers who never experienced the struggle and passion of 2014, mostly new faces who signed up for entirely different motives, soldiers who didn't feel the grief and the camaraderie from the beginning. New faces who arrived from that disconnected peace life. But what else could she do except stay? What could any of them do? How could they simply walk away with ease when it was still unresolved, when it was right next door? When some of their comrades from the beginning were still out there fighting and dying? When everything they risked so much for and lost so much for loomed above in a forgotten cloud, as if it were all for nothing?

I went to take a shower. I stood there for forty minutes under hot water, crying and picking pieces of my friends out of my hair. I just wanted to shave my head and wash it all away.

"What were you doing before Maidan, what was your life like? Why did you go?"

Her answer was so simple during our first interview. The propaganda. The Russian media outlets. The "official" reportage of Maidan. It didn't make sense to her, the stories that Ukrainians were murdering citizens simply for speaking Russian, the native tongue for almost all in post-Soviet countries. The stories that Ukrainians were slaughtering children, that they were on their way, marching into Moscow, bloodthirsty to overthrow the capital and oppress the population. She wanted to prove it wasn't true. But it was more than that. She wanted to be a part of the truth.

Valkyrie was drawn to the fire she saw in the Maidan revolutionaries. Drawn to their strength in fighting for something they believed in, against the corruption, against the greed and oppression of their leaders. Fighting against the same corruption and oppression she lived under in Russia, that I imagine she dreamed of fighting one day in a revolution of her own. The same corruption that killed her father, only months before the Maidan began. And in visiting the aftermath of the revolution's victory in Kyiv, when it took an unexpected turn into a new war, that fire, that purpose she was drawn to became one that she could also fight for. It became her purpose.

I never felt that the wars I had been sent into were unresolved on a personal level, even though they were clearly far from over when I left. I never felt a need to go back to Afghanistan or Iraq to continue fighting until the end, because I didn't know what the end was supposed to look like. Because the wars I was sent into, they weren't really my wars. They were someone else's.

THE LESSER EVIL

"The local warlords have invited us to attend a welcome feast to-night, and all leadership on ground *will* attend," First Sergeant said.

"Mandatory fun," he added with a smirk.

No one liked mandatory fun. It usually wasn't fun, and it wasn't what you preferred to be doing on your time off, and that's exactly when it was always scheduled. Like a Battalion Ball on a Saturday night, and instead of hitting the town with your peers, you'd have to put on your blues and pretend you liked talking to high-ranking officers and NCOs. But this, having to attend a feast with warlords in the middle of a combat zone in Afghanistan, was an entire new echelon of mandatory fun. A warlord didn't exactly sound like the kind of person I'd venture to have a get-together with in general, and anyway, were they supposed to be the good guys?

"Not really, but we gotta make nice so we can stay here," said Renaud, my platoon sergeant, and I wouldn't understand much more than that before the seventeen of us comprising "leadership on ground" walked in a gaggle up the road to where a large circus tent was set up for the occasion.

It fit the idea of what a feast might look like, made festive by the bright yellow and red oriental patterned sheets of the tent's ceiling and walls and by the red and white rugs that covered the floor from end to end. It felt festive by sound and smell also, with traditional Afghan music coming from giant, outdated speakers and the aroma of the feast wafting from the long, narrow table weighed down with large dishes, bowls and platters stacked high with varieties of fruits, vegetables and meats. Outside of that, the entire thing was just bizarre—even comedic in its own way—like we were walking

45

into some kind of war satire theatrical performance, act one opening with our arrival, dressed for the party in full combat uniform, flak jackets, Kevlar, gas masks, loaded weapons and all, just standing there awkwardly while strangers we knew absolutely nothing about stared from every corner of the tent.

It's not that I expected the Army to provide extensive background details on the whys of most situations we were sent into, but they usually at least had a protocol or a policy, a laundry list of dos and don'ts for just about everything. Not this time. There wasn't a formal introduction when we walked inside. Nor was there any kind of advance briefing on who would be there or what might happen. We didn't know who the warlords were, what they looked like, or if they were even in attendance. Here we were, the special guests of the feast wearing our standard US desert fatigues like flashing neon lights in a dark room. But the Afghans were anything but uniform in their appearance, wearing everything from various versions of military formals and fatigues to the traditional Pashtun-style garments of loose-fitting blouses and trousers, tunics, scarves and turbans, to the few who wore regular, westernized civilian clothing. There was no telling who was what in the room, or if there was even a common belief shared among them all.

The only clear guidance outside of knowing that we had to show up, with the implied task of playing nice, was that we shouldn't eat anything raw or uncooked. Apparently, either some people didn't get that memo or their eagerness to consume something beside the MREs we'd been living on for three meals a day fortified them with the courage to risk the situation … and to spend the next two days with food poisoning, hooked up to IVs.

So that was it. Show up, play nice with the warlords we couldn't even identify, don't eat the cherries and look good for the Afghan camera crews who were zeroing in on the best of awkward situations. And that was just about every situation in the tent where there was an attempted interaction between the Afghans and the Americans. On one side of the tent, metal chairs in rows faced inward toward each other, paired in twos as if they were tables for two without the tables. A speed dating type of situation reserved

for an American soldier and an Afghan to sit down and eat together while attempting to communicate through the language barrier
as a video camera put the spotlight on them from a few feet away.
Or the best of moments, the Afghans who wanted to dance with
the Americans; this is where my wonder of a shared belief became
clearer.

With curious stares and smiles, one by one they gravitated toward us as we tried to navigate the food situation and the feast in
general, eventually forming a small huddle around us. As the music
turned to a new song, the volume increased and a few of them ges-
tured for us to follow their lead into a spacious central area of the
tent where they began to demonstrate the movements and motions
of what appeared to be a traditional Afghan dance.

I backed up and watched from the sideline while a few others
played along, trying to mimic the expressive arm motions while
their M4s and M16s bounced clumsily against their backs. The
men gracefully weaved across the floor, gliding in and around them
in circles, one even falling to his knees in a hypnotic and dramatic
phase of the dance.

The dancing was the main attraction of the tent. The Americans,
seated in their own section opposite the mingling area, watched in
amusement. The individuals gathered around the dancing clapped
along and laughed cheerily. But there was a different kind of energy
coming from the background, from the Afghans who were seated
and standing along the edges of the tent, keeping to themselves as
they watched over these interactions and us. It came most strongly
from the section designated for their VIPs, judging by the air of
prestige and formality surrounding them. Their varied uniforms
were more distinguished and decorated, their posture and eyes
still, stoic and intimidating. A few wore white, formal, long-sleeved
military-style coats with black shoulder lapels of rank. They glared
with cold, disapproving stares. I'm pretty sure they were the warlords.

LEAFLETS IN THE SKY

I HAVE PLENTY OF PICTURES FROM THE FEAST. Of the men dancing, the platters of food, the video camera strobe lights, the soldiers in varieties of uniform: the solid olive drab and camouflage forest pixels, the semiformal greens and visor caps with red bands. I have pictures of the white tunics, the Northern Alliance Pakol hats, the stoic faces framed by steel bushels of facial hair projected by the contrast of crisp, formal white uniforms.

After my military service, after coming down from the freedom of civilian life, when my brain finally calibrated into the mindset of wanting to understand, I researched the empty explanations that were never given to us. Who were the warlords that we had to "make nice" with? What did they represent? Who were the array of selected participants attending the feast? I searched for evidence that this feast existed beyond my photographs and our memories of it. I wanted to know where the recorded footage from the video cameras was published, how we were presented to the public's eye and how we may have become the subjects of propaganda, propaganda like the images we printed on paper leaflets and dropped from the sky over Afghanistan's population, a psychological sway to the side of the "good guys," the American forces. To the side of a lesser evil.

In time, the photographs revealed so much more than I noticed in the moment of taking them. In the midst of the crowded chaos in the tent, the little Afghan boys blending in seamlessly in the background and foreground of each frame, almost like an attached limb to the Afghan men they stood or sat next to, and always without expression. And the men dancing with my comrades, I noticed how perhaps some of them weren't really dancing with my comrades but rather dancing for the men of status watching on. The presence of the boys, and then the younger men dancing, their placement in the center of the tent and their movements, so many details mimicked what I would later understand as the practice of *bacha bazi*, a custom in Afghanistan often involving sexual slavery and prostitution of young males or boys, called "dancing boys," by older and powerful men.

Leaflets in the sky.

In time, I would also understand that the most prominent figure at the feast was a former warlord and the newly appointed governor of Kandahar. He wasn't one of the men in the formal white uniforms. But I found him there in one of my photographs, ironically dressed in more westernized and nontraditional clothing, surrounded by the video cameras. Gul Agha Sherzai, the former Mujahideen commander who fought against the Soviet invasion of Afghanistan. The same Mujahideen commander that ousted the Soviets from their country with the support of the United States. The same Mujahideen commander who fought alongside the alleged greatest evil of 9/11, Osama bin Laden, the reason we were sent to Kandahar.

The lesser evil. Leaflets in the sky. I still have a handful of them, war trophies, souvenirs from those first few weeks on the ground. On one, there's a photograph of an al-Qaeda man senselessly whipping a woman in a burqa. Underneath, "Is this the future you want for your women and children?" printed in Pashto and Dari. The underlying psychological message: The United States is here to free you from these evils.

Perception is reality. One of my commanders in Afghanistan used to say it all the time, and it truly pissed me off every time he said it. Because I didn't expect it to be the same in a war zone, this driving force behind the military's culture. That the value of the image always seemed to outweigh the value of truth, and the truth was often a complete mockery of the public's perception. A perfect example: West Point, the statue of George Washington riding his horse on the apron of the academy, the spectacle of all visitors to photograph the prestige from a distance. It's the postcard image of the academy, the visual of "Duty, Honor, Country" during the parades, the cadets standing in formation in silence, surrounding the statue in the position of attention, parade rest or ordering arms: George Washington on his horse, leading America's revolutionaries into battle and onward to victory, riding off the apron and toward the glory of the public watching from the bleachers.

The view is quite different from the other side. What do the cadets see? George Washington's backside and his horse's ass. And as we stand there within the ranks of this perfect and prestigious formation, stoic and facing the crowds, our eyes scan from left to right, hunting for a wobbling cadet with weak knees as we place wagers in whispers over who's going to pass out first.

In Afghanistan, the reality is that we were required to submit award recommendations, the Army Commendation Medals and the highly sought-after combat zone Bronze Star Medals and Silver Star Medals, before we even began our mission or did anything worthy of receiving an award outside of just being there in harm's way. The reality is that plenty of decisions were made based on adding promotion-worthy war zone bullet points to the highest-ranking officer and non-commissioned officer evaluation reports, and often these decisions were not in the best interests of their soldiers. The reality is that many of the prisoners brought to the detainee camp my platoon was charged to build, the prisoners who walked blindly with potato sacks over their heads, pushed from behind with the nozzles of AKs, the prisoners who were seen as "rag heads" by eighteen-year-olds without enough education, were wrongly imprisoned, and some continue to sit in prison to this day.

The reality is that many of us believed that our presence there was saving an oppressed population from the Taliban and promoting humanity. But we did this by committing crimes against humanity and allying with powers who committed crimes against humanity in plain sight. The reality is that once we hit the ground, before I even had a chance to conceptualize what I understand today, my own perception of my purpose dissolved into this reality: I didn't feel an invested purpose in our country's mission there, so I simply repurposed my mission. It became about making it through the days and taking care of my comrades and soldiers until we got home. It became about simply staying alive.

ULIYA "CUBA" SIDOROVA

TRANSLATED EXCERPT FROM INTERVIEW
AVDIIVKA, UKRAINE, 2018

*We took the wounded into the concert hall, so they could be
transferred to the hospital. What I remember from this moment
is that when we came out, there were three or four Berkut
officers who were burning a Ukrainian flag. They set it on fire
and were laughing. And then I was taken outside the Maidan
territory. And what I remember from the time we were leaving is
how much blood I saw, how many badly injured people. But life
outside of Maidan was just business as usual. I come in and see
people drinking beer. And that is just five minutes from Maidan.
And everybody's life is just like before.*

Peace Life Problems

August 2019
Popasna, Ukraine

"And what about being home? Filth, selfishness, people wanting to fool each other, rob each other, fatten their wallets. So many vague problems. They put flags on their balconies and proclaim themselves patriots. Now everyone's wearing vyshyvankas or speaking Ukrainian. There was a jerk last year who told me, 'Why do you speak the invaders' language?' I mean, Gagauz language, Chinese language, whatever language ... there are things you just can't understand," Valera resentfully concluded, his silence giving way to the sound of Luhansk Oblast's forest birds and the crackling of wood and ember as the soldier behind him stirred a giant iron pot of soup over an open fire. But even when Valera spoke, his deep, soothing voice only added to the perfect lullaby of the environment surrounding us, this proven by his comrade Sasha, who continued unfazed in a deep afternoon nap, lying on a tarp on the forest floor nearby, his armored personnel carrier (APC) parked in the brush, a stray puppy, much like I'd see at all frontline positions, tucked deep into his armpit, joining him in the cadence of sleep.

Valera continued in silent contemplation, elbow on the ground, head resting on his hand near my small Tascam recorder. He was barefooted and sprawled out on a different tarp where we conducted our interview, the interview I'd been chasing for more than a year, ever since I met him.

"The driver said the faster you drive, the smaller the holes get," Babay had said the day before from the front passenger seat of a taxi as we clocked well over 150 kilometers per hour down a thin stretch of Donbas highway, dodging holes and the disorderly paths of cars traveling in the opposite direction at the same high speed. Icon dangling from the rearview mirror, Euro music pulsed through the metal frame of a *Back-to-the-Future*-style car with a ravenous werewolf painted across the entire hood, the music's vibration buzzed through my body from the side door and onto the three passengers squashed to my right, who anchored all but the whiplash.

Only in the Donbas would something like this become a norm in my life. Having no need for a fixer anymore, just taking a taxi to the front line, bypassing commanders, press officers and checkpoints on back roads, getting dropped off outside a forest on a desolate highway in Popasna where Valera's squad, camouflaged in the brush, manned their APCs.

I originally met him in the peace life with Valkyrie, both of them arriving at my flat in Kyiv late one night, coming straight off the train from the front line for a few days of leave. He was another of the 2014 Aidar veterans, but even more specifically, he was one of three comprising Valkyrie's APC team (all three claimed to have been the APC commander) and now continued his service in renewed contracts with the Ukrainian Armed Forces.

"He said he doesn't have a problem with the Russians. They're just misunderstood," Babay translated for Valera on a balcony overwhelmed with cigarette smoke and 30mm ammunition shells, 2014 war trophies, stuffed and spilling over with discarded butts. His statement was just about the last I'd understand before his loyal interpreting skills and comprehension of English evaporated in whiskey and a conversation that carried on well into the night and without me, even though the topic was a product of my own instigation. A product of my desire to understand the "fuck the Russians" mentality that often found bold placement in my interviews, this blanketed hate toward an entire population for simply living on the other side of a border, whether soldier or civilian.

Even within the interview stories that conveyed an empathetic memory for a Russian soldier or a Russian family member caught up on the other side, it's as if these words, spoken impulsively and without premeditation, had to be immediately countered and covered up with something crass and over the top to make up for a brief moment of humanity. Naturally, the topic reemerged during our evening gatherings, often sparked by my devil's advocate punches from the perspective of an outsider, or sometimes by my reaction to a snarky side jab that I chose to learn Russian before Ukrainian when often they had been speaking Russian just moments earlier. Not to mention that fifty percent of my recorded interviews thus far were spoken in Russian, even the "fuck the Russians" parts. And then to complete the irony in it all, there was Valkyrie, standing right there in the middle of the "fuck the Russians," totally unfazed, mind you, as if she weren't Russian herself.

"Then what about Valkyrie?"

She's not really Russian. She's from West Russia; it's like Ukraine.

Valkyrie's different. She doesn't count.

If they were like her, they'd already be fighting on our side. They had their chance.

Fuck the Russians.

A reminder of the "fuckin' Hajis" and "fuckin' rag heads" that took all but twelve hours to crack into the air and then into every other sentence in Afghanistan, which then prevailed well throughout Iraq, most often (but not always) from the fresh soldiers who knew nothing beyond a mandatory thirty-minute culture and sensitivity briefing as part of our pre-deployment process. A briefing, most often slept through, to check the box of government requirements. A briefing with a PowerPoint slideshow of what not to do to piss off the "other" people, a briefing seemingly designed to protect the American government's property rather than installing any kind of understanding or respect for the people in the land we'd disrupt. Except it was different for the Ukrainians; they weren't disrupting another country's land.

"Fuck the Russians."

Valera went against the grain.

From the tarp on the forest floor, I asked him: "Will you expand on something you said when I first met you? You said Russians are not all bad, but just misunderstood." Babay interpreted.

"I am still good towards the Russians," he said. "They are the people like us. They're military people. It's their job. They are given an order; they obey it. If a soldier denies obeying an order, there's only one way in Russia—jail, jail, jail. These soldiers have families, children, they understand they have no choice. They chose to be military men and that's it. There is a problem with those who give orders. Not with those who execute them."

Perhaps there was a difference. Between the volunteers who left the war since the peace agreements in 2015 and those who remained on in official contracts and experienced the trials of being a soldier in a government-controlled military, when decisions were no longer made from the heart of the individual, but by an entity of generals and politicians responding to global politics and agendas far beyond the ground soldiers' understanding or concern. An entity that often waged deals with a lesser evil to achieve a purpose in a greater game, a purpose that often disregarded the outcome of the soldiers fighting for it.

Man in the Store

Reflection on April 2003
Nasiriyah, Iraq

In Iraq, I had disposable cameras and a digital camera. When I'd lead our convoys back into Kuwait for supply runs, I'd jump on a computer in the headquarters tent and email photos home to family and friends. Once I even sent a few to *National Geographic* with a message to the editor: these are photos from the ground, from one soldier's perspective, photos that captured real moments in time and could answer the questions I knew people would ask of me when I returned. Photos that showed the other side of mainstream, sensationalized media I remembered airing on the small television we eventually acquired in our operations tent in Afghanistan.

The editor responded a few days later with a kind dismissal that I more than likely would have never received if I hadn't been a soldier serving in the war.

The photographs were mostly of the people. As if I were a tourist and not at war, trying to find normalcy in the situation. So many of the images represented what I wanted to believe in the moment of taking them, hoping that an individual could make a difference, be more than just a representative of those who sent us there. Strangely, when looking at the photos years later, some of them tell so much more of a story than I was able to conceptualize in the moment of taking them, the crowds and the children flocking around us in the streets of Nasiriyah, the children on the side of the road when we first crossed the border.

I can still hear the stones popping under our tires and clinking back up against the metal of our Humvees and trucks as we slowly rolled across the border from Kuwait and through the first sign of a village. Slow motion, sand. Everything was the color of sand, blanketed by a sandy haze. Through the haze, shapes began to emerge. Lopsided huts made from sticks and thatched reeds for roofing, laundry lines of clothing blowing in the wind. I was waiting for grenades and mortars to rain down on us, but that's not what happened at all. Instead, children began to emerge, barefoot and running beside our vehicles—a little girl in a violet dress, waving and squinting against the sand blowing into her eyes, a little boy in red and blue stripes giving the thumbs up, a boy standing at the position of attention, holding the American salute and not dropping it until we passed.

The last photograph I took of the people in the streets, of the crowds surrounding us, was the day that changed the way I would later perceive most of the photographs I had taken before. Maybe the children in the photographs with their hands waving in the air weren't greeting us but were asking for money or food. And the boy saluting, maybe he wasn't saluting out of respect for America or why we were there, but simply playing curiously, or even gathering information to be used against us. And in the photograph of children on the streets, past the playful smiles and thumbs ups, I see what I didn't see through the lens in that moment: the children farther back, their hands in a gesture of shooting us with pistols.

~

"Sometimes I wake up under my bed, looking for my weapon," Fernandez said. It was nearly ten years since we had deployed to Iraq together, yet this was the first time we ever talked about it.

"I also have nightmares about the man in the store."

We were together that day, on a routine trip into downtown Nasiriyah to meet Hussein, our Iraqi contractor, at his shop in the center of the city. I was outside the store taking pictures with a disposable camera; the children were smiling and laughing as usual, pushing each other to squeeze into the frame. I remember the sound of bells jingling behind me as a door opened, and how the cheering slowly quieted to silence as the crowd's eyes wandered over my shoulder.

He was an older man, standing in the store's doorway with a book clutched firmly in one hand and prayer beads dangling from the other. Staring directly at us, he began to preach in Arabic, his tone blanketing the entire street into silence, commanding the attention of every living presence.

"Things are meant to be the way they are! You should not be here!" he concluded in English, the last words trailed by an absolute silence, an uncomfortable silence before the crowd broke into applause and then into a cheer. But as soon as the man retreated into his store and the bells jingled with the closing of the door, the crowd directed their attention back to us, now through Hussein's store window, slapping and knocking against the glass playfully as if nothing had happened.

"Why was I still outside?" I asked Fernandez. Because before we spoke about it, I assumed she was standing there with me when this happened. I hadn't realized she was already inside Hussein's shop, that I was the only soldier left standing there in the streets when the man appeared. I didn't realize that she didn't hear the English words that I heard the man say so clearly: "You should not be here!"

"You used to bring candy to the children," she answered, something else I'd forgotten. It puts me back in the memory again, playing with the children, buying prayer beads, giving out candy, but something feels different this time. I'm not comfortable, and instead of the playful raise-the-roof gestures I thought I remembered from the children, I only hear them shrieking, "Saddam Hussein, Saddam Hussein," and they're pushing one another to stand in front of me, pantomiming the cutting of their throats by sliding their fingers slowly across their necks. "Saddam Hussein!"

I push through the crowd, away from the street where the Humvee is parked, and I see the glass door opening and the desert-camouflaged backs of my comrades as they walk inside Hussein's shop, and I'm only a few feet behind them, but it feels like miles against the pressure of the crowds. The shop bells jingle, like old cow bells, and the busy sound of a crowded street gets lower in slow motion, almost as if someone's holding the knob on a volume switch, slowly turning it to silence. Eyes wander behind me. I turn, and then I see the man, his weathered face, his white and gray beard, his pale-blue eyes staring at me, or they had to be blue, because how else could they be so piercing, so cold? How else could they burn right through me?

He's walking slowly toward me, thrusting the book forward with his hand, each motion accenting the closing word of a phrase in an enraged sermon. He pauses, his eyes lock on mine, and I know he sees my fear. It's fueling his anger; it's fueling his words, and I can't hear anything else now, only his voice, his voice and some kind of buzzing, the buzz of a large wasp or a bee, and I brace myself, for at any moment the buzzing will give way to a massive fire, heat, a deafening explosion, and then I won't hear his voice anymore. I won't hear the buzzing, and maybe I'll die so quickly that I won't feel anything.

A hand on my shoulder pulls me into the shop, and the man is outside the door now, still staring through the glass, preaching, screaming, the crowds behind him watching in silence while Hussein fumbles to close the door and locks it. And now, for the first time in more than ten years, I can hear Fernandez's desperate voice behind me, "What is he saying? What is he saying?"

Even back then, in that moment, as I silently backed away from the man, I wanted to tell him that I agreed, that I too felt we should not be on their land. But I was on their land. I wore the uniform, and that's how I would be defined by the people: an invader, a target, an American, a curiosity, a miscalculated hope, a soldier of the United States Army and everything the uniform represented—the things that we didn't even understand we represented.

ENEMY IN THE PEACE LIFE

JULY 2019
KYIV, UKRAINE

I couldn't stop it. Trotsky reached into the black pouch around his waist before extending his open palm toward Valkyrie and me, an offering of two shield-shaped tablets. Not even a moment to ask what it was, to look closer, to understand what was happening before she snatched one of them up. Her hand moved directly from his hand to her mouth as she walked backward, swallowing it with a look of satisfaction, as if she wanted me to know that she understood the repercussions, that it was a bad decision, an intentional moment of self-destruction. She wanted me to know that there was nothing I could do about it.

She went somewhere dark, a black hole of isolation. Not only during the hours before that moment, when we were sitting on a flat balcony with Trotsky, but for the previous two months. It had been a strange summer of silence after what had been constant, daily communication.

"She's depressed," Trotsky explained on the balcony, volunteering as an unwanted interpreter. Not unwanted because I didn't like him or because his level of English was exhausting to decipher, but because he had a strange way of distorting the conversation, sometimes steering it into his own probing then coveting the answers to my questions, and sometimes falling away into his own dialogue within the topic of my inquiry that carried on without me. All variants resulted in one thing: a dark cloud of confusion and misunderstanding within the language barrier, such as it did on this night with Valkyrie.

Trotsky, often referred to as "fuckin' Trotsky," was an eternal challenge, a coveter of dark secrets, the veteran who'd agree to a meeting and then vanish for months before casually resurfacing, never offering an explanation for leaving his friends swirling in a panic that he might be lying dead in a ditch somewhere.

The darkness and mystery worked when it came to the game of chasing after an interview, which may have been his intention. But I had already decided to pursue a recorded story with him, ever since the night of the martial law declaration. After we dropped Valkyrie off at the train station to return to the front line, he got into a raging argument with the taxi driver on the way back to the flat.

"He doesn't believe that there is a war still happening," Trotsky concluded as he slammed the door on the driver's closing remarks. The situation brought clarity to what I'd only heard about in almost all of the interviews but had never seen in real-time: this plague the war veterans in Kyiv and all cities away from eastern Ukraine faced when attempting to integrate back into the civilian world. If you didn't fight the war, you were forced to be part of a population that didn't acknowledge the war existed.

Trotsky and Valkyrie often stuck together in the peace life, at least during the times she returned from the front line. That was nothing unusual for the 2014 veteran tribe, craving familiar ground, which even I found in their world. But over time I noticed how the two of them in particular became quite toxic together, and more than in the average, weekend-warrior type of way. It was as if their primary common ground was a darkness they each harbored, but Trotsky seemed to do more than simply gravitate toward darkness. It's almost as if he needed it, even craved it, and while it seemed he had no ambition to escape it, he also didn't want to be left alone. So he walked like a black hole, sucking the most vulnerable into his abyss, including me; many nights with him concluded with my sobbing in some inexplicable sadness he found a way to expose.

"She wants to let go and have fun tonight," he said, in response to my perplexed expression as Valkyrie laced up her boots and threw on her jacket, a clear sign that there wouldn't be further probing or resolution in my quest to understand this new, unfamiliar turbulence that hovered all around her. Instead, a plan transpired between them, circling around me by way of the language barrier, placing me in the back of a taxicab en route to an off-the-grid, pop-up weekend rave in a tucked-away Kyiv neighborhood. Valkyrie once made a comment that when she was only fifteen years old, she had been a well-practiced party thrower in Russia, planning events such as this. It was a statement that presented pages worth of new curiosities and questions about a past I would learn in bits and pieces, maybe over decades rather than months or years, or quite possibly never.

I knew there was so much more to her story than what she revealed during her interview. Something raw and vulnerable, how could there not be with the life she lived up until this point? I was amazed by the trust that had been placed in me by so many of the volunteers I'd interviewed. I didn't need to push or pry; they offered a glimpse into some of their deepest truths, some that would stay eternally confidential. But Valkyrie, who I spent more time with than most, deflected exposing weakness as if she wore osteoderms.

"Don't drink too much," she told me from the back seat, in a beyond-intoxicated state. I laughed at the irony and irrationality, because it would have been a perfect joke had she meant it that way. I'd just watched her down nearly an entire bottle of vermouth. But she just looked toward me and then past me with a blank expression, as if she had no recollection of what she'd already consumed, no recollection of anything before that moment. There was only the present, but apparently even the present was not enough.

"Trotsky, what the fuck was that?" I asked. But his only response was an amused expression and a shrug of his shoulders as we both watched her slip away to the DJ table, getting lost in the music, dancing in isolation. And for the first time, I felt like a visitor in their world.

There was nothing I could do to steer the situation, no rationality to offer. All I could do was watch and wait for the next chapter to unfold in this choose-your-own-ending book, pray your last choice didn't lead to the fall off-the-cliff, sudden-death closer page. And then the page turned.

Valkyrie stopped dancing, noticing Trotsky and me and the recently arrived Babay gathered nearby. She walked over to us, resting against the stone wall where I sat. Leaning over, head down, she reached her hands into her hair, combing through it, flipping it back, rocking back and forth in the alternate reality she was surviving within. It took her to the ground, foam fizzing from her mouth and onto the bricks. Others ran over, some watching and others helping to lift her from the ground, a masked Valkyrie with protruding eyes, protruding lips where her teeth bit through, a wild animal flapping her arms to fly away, to defend herself, a rabid animal grabbing my forearm as I tried to stabilize her on her feet, and sinking her teeth in, drawing blood.

"What the fuck did you give her?" I asked Trotsky once again, as we closed the door to the taxicab.

"I took one too, Jenn, and I'm fine. I don't feel anything," Babay said from the front seat of the cab. And I also took a small piece of one. Just a corner, a sampling of curiosity. *I'll go where you go, but not all the way.* But the only thing I felt was a dire need to clench my fists, and it felt good to clench them. Tight. I clenched them in a way I'd never felt before.

~

The scar on my forearm was a reminder of what Valkyrie carried inside. The rage. The emptiness. A darkness. The distress over the choice she knew she had to make, to leave the Army and become a mother to her daughter, or to go on like this for the rest of her life.

I knew that letting go had to be terrifying. It meant breaking free of the image she wanted to hold onto, being the legendary Russian heroine of the volunteer warriors, the Russian who fought for Ukraine. It meant confronting the reality of her losses and wounds, multiple brain injuries and layers of trauma that would be shrugged off by military-funded state psychologists with an array of numbing Soviet-era medications. Letting go meant abandoning the only purpose she felt she carried, or maybe the only purpose she felt capable of carrying. Letting go meant coming to terms with the reality that she had no family outside the war zone. Her father was still dead, her daughter a stranger in her life, and the rest were on the other side of a border she could never cross again, unless she wanted to be killed or go to prison.

In the war zone, she was someone, and she belonged. But in the peace life, not only was she displaced by her experience in war, but she was also a Russian who still wouldn't be granted Ukrainian citizenship, five years after crossing the border. Not until she fulfilled the outdated, bureaucratic requirements of gathering documents from her mother country, proving she was clear of criminal history. A mother country that Ukraine was at war with, that already considered her a criminal for fighting against it.

Valkyrie. She was the heroine who was good enough to serve as a soldier in the Ukrainian Armed Forces, who was good enough to be awarded medals from the president, who was good enough to die for Ukraine, but who wasn't good enough to be Ukrainian.

It became clear that proximity didn't play a role in separating the two worlds. That it didn't take traveling over oceans, over continents, back to a faraway land called home. It simply took being confronted with a population completely separated from her experiences. A population who harbored enemies that weren't expected in the peace life.

VASYL ANTONIAK

TRANSLATED EXCERPT FROM INTERVIEW
KYIV, UKRAINE, 2018

There was a moment when winter came and when I finally made my way out of there. We went to Kyiv with Taras for the New Year. He left me at a railway station. It was four or five a.m. so I slept a few hours on my backpack and then decided to go into the city and down to the subway dressed in my uniform and with my military backpack. Then I saw all those crowds of people moving around and they really pissed me off. And I couldn't understand what was going on as a day ago I was basically in the war zone and then I was in a completely different place, a different reality. I wanted to kill all those people as I really felt out of place.

One day I was in Shchastia and the next morning I was in Kyiv. There was no consecutive change of understanding. Maybe if I had gone by train, it would have been different as it would have been a softer transition to the new reality.

THE POINT OF LETTING GO

AUGUST 2002
BAGRAM, AFGHANISTAN

It was the day we left Afghanistan. The day of reaching that arbitrary finish line that we were perpetually counting down the days to reach. Arbitrary because it was never a concrete date, only a vicious cycle of hopes and letdowns, of speculations spanning over the course of months. Until two days earlier, when we finally received the official word from Captain Dunbar that we had a bird with our name on it.

There was no need to sleep the night before. Instead, we journeyed up to the flight line with our duffel bags and rucksacks, leaving the blown-out bathhouse in Bagram that we'd been living in for the last time. We were determined to witness the C-17's approach from over the summit of the rock-clipped mountains that seemed to scrape the sky, to watch its wheels touch the ground of the airstrip, the same C-17 that at sunrise would take us up and away and out of that place forever.

Captain Dunbar snapped a photo with my camera as we posed together outside the waiting area tent, standing with our M16s and M4s, each wrapped in plastic to prevent an additional disassembly and cleaning of dust and sand from the metal crevices later on. Smiling, we stood in front of the HESCO bastions that barricaded the runway behind us, and behind them, our lone C-17 taxied along, its engines whining a high-pitched song against the night, trapped in by the mountains, this giant gray beast of a military cargo plane shadowed against a deep orange and blue saturated sky of a morning on the rise.

Dunbar was happy for us. It was our turn, the last eight of us from Bravo Company on the ground, we were finally going home. She and I had gotten to know each other well over the previous month as I practically lived inside her "office," the small Movement Control Team tent adjacent to the flight line, hounding her for space on every incoming cargo flight to squeeze another group of soldiers or a piece of equipment on board until all 140 of us and our heavy engineering vehicles were off the ground and heading back home. I was in there so damn much, crowding the already too-small space, that she propped up a giant paper pad on an easel to field incoming phone calls and visits on my behalf. "LT Blatty's Message Board," it said at the top, and below that the bulleted notes ranged anywhere from "2 PAX, 1 Dozer on Flight BL760" to "Get the Sheryl Crow CD off my desk. Now."

It was a light week leading up to that day, our only final obligation to sit there and wait for news of a designated bird to lift us away. Time was spent smack talking nonsense and listing the "first thing I'm gonna do" when I get back, most often revolving around food, alcohol and sex. There was freedom in the air with the top brass gone, and Specialist Diggles took the most advantage of it, knowing well enough that I wouldn't reprimand him for his hair that had grown too long or for sporting his heavy metal, ripped-sleeve black T-shirt outside of our sleeping quarters during the day.

One night, on running through my own "when I get back" list, which involved taking my motorcycle out for a spin down Highway 204 to Tybee Island, he immediately grabbed a sheet of lined paper and wrote out a hand-scribbled will in my name, relinquishing my bike to him, should something happen before we got out of there—just in case.

Sure, a joke, but it's almost as if we were waiting for that kind of dark irony to unfold, that something might happen to us at the very last minute, because it was too hard to believe that any of it was real, that we were actually going home. It was about as tangible as when we had left Savannah seven months before, this surreal feeling of time and space opening and closing within the blink of an eye. Exiting one planet and jumping to the next, like we had never left in the first place and it was all just a dream, but then knowing that we had to have left, because there was no other way to quantify all that happened in the space between.

I was still hovering in that space on the final flight home from Frankfurt to Savannah. We were on a commercial airplane for the first time, reclining in real seats, our weapons stored in the belly of the aircraft, and as I sat there listening to a mix I had made before leaving home, I tried putting myself back there on the other side, thinking about everything that I left—the people, the friends and family, the rituals and relationships and the expectations of a fast-moving world. And then something happened. The excitement of going home just fizzled out of me with an exhalation left somewhere in the air over the Atlantic. I didn't know how to feel any more or what I was supposed to feel. Because I didn't feel anything. I wasn't happy. I wasn't sad. I just ... was.

The Woman in the Abaya

THERE ARE SOME PHOTOGRAPHS FROM IRAQ that remain unaltered. My perception hasn't changed over the years when I look at them; it's as if I'm still standing there in the moment of snapping the shutter, living the same moment again, a moment when I'm not just an observer documenting another culture: the earthen huts, the barefooted women shepherding cows through the sweltering summer sand, the protests in the city streets. Or when I'm not documenting how our presence altered the landscape and energy of the people, like the children crowding around us in the streets, the little boy saluting on the side of the road. Instead, in these unaltered photographs, I'm standing within the landscape and with the people. They are photographs anyone can look at and walk away with a universal memory, as if they are the ones who snapped the shutter.

When we went on our supply runs in Nasiriyah, we'd always stop at a building on the outskirts of the city to pick up our translator, Yassir, before meeting Hussein at his shop. They always warned us to be careful when the locals flocked around the Humvee, especially Yassir. He was perpetually worried that we would become targets. But once while we were waiting for him, I snapped a photograph through the open window frame of the vehicle, of a woman who approached me, wearing an abaya. She wasn't threatened when I held up the camera; in fact, she looked directly through it as if it were invisible, holding my gaze and smiling as if we'd known each other for years, as if we were about to embark on a long conversation over the ins and outs of our lives since we'd last seen each other. For just that moment, I forgot that I was wearing the uniform, that I was armed, that I was in Iraq. I forgot that she was wearing an abaya or that we spoke different languages and came from different worlds. In that moment, we were just two humans standing on the same piece of earth at the same moment. There was nothing different between us.

That was the unintentional photograph, the kind I'd later believe could tell a story in its truest form. But in time I realized that even a photograph, as unintentional as it might be in the moment of taking it, can be distorted. It can fall subject to a variety of interpretations. It can be used to tell or to supplement someone else's story, thus altering a perception or a truth that might have been seen without it. It can be manipulated and even edited to alter a scene into a new reality. But the eyes, this point of human connection when the camera becomes invisible even in plain sight, they cannot be easily manipulated.

FOR THE FAMILY

Valera's portrait in Popasna was the epitome of unintentional. I took it forty-five minutes after the "formal" photo session, after standing him in front of the black blanket while a few of his comrades watched over this tactical studio rigged in the middle of a forest. After telling him, without much confidence, that I had what I needed.

Babay knew me well. He sensed the camera going back up, felt the energy change, something more comparable to the previous night, when we'd had downtime around a fire, recording uninhibited and informal stories.

Sitting on a tree stump, Valera picked up the two stray puppies who had taken up temporary residence at their positions. Babay, still carrying the blanket from the breakdown, stretched it behind him, his long arms extending almost wide enough to fill the entire frame and avoid a future cropping of the forest behind. It was the only horizontal portrait in the New York exhibit.

The director of the institute there had tried to remove the placard with Valera's quotation about not carrying hatred for all Russian soldiers. When I questioned why it was missing from the wall next to the portrait, he claimed it might upset some of the visitors. I won the debate to display it, but it was still a vivid reminder not only of the secondary war that was taking place in the United States, such as no Russian journalists being allowed at the opening for an interview, but also a reminder that this was a Ukrainian organization hosting the event. And just like the first project opening in Chicago the year before, the guests would likely be dominated by the Ukrainian diaspora, an audience that my project couldn't succeed without, that it welcomed with open arms, but one that my project's message wasn't designed to reach in the United States. They already knew about the war; they were emotionally connected and invested in its outcome, seemingly even more than those who populated Ukraine's peace life.

"Thank you for telling the stories of these heroes," a woman standing next to me had said during the Chicago opening. We were watching a multimedia video of documentary photography and audio to supplement the portraits and text story excerpts when suddenly, a cell phone snapshot of a memorial bust in Kyiv flipped past.

"This was my friend's son," she continued.

I was surprised the photo made its way into the video; I must have accidentally thrown it into the jumble of extra footage I rushed over to the journalist who volunteered to create it. But I remembered taking it, in 2018, during a walk around Kyiv's university campus with Babay. He took a rare slow down to pause and point it out to me, a plaque affixed to the side of a building; a giant bust of a youthful face struggling to age into the bronze of history. Beneath it was an inscription of his name, his year of birth and year of death, and that he had died protecting Ukraine.

Not much was said at the time, just a mention that he was in Babay's platoon, followed by something about "controversy" before Babay changed the subject and continued his always-in-a-hurry walking pace, made even more impossible to keep up with by the giant strides of his six-foot-two frame. It wasn't until a few months later, before the opening in Chicago and after too many whiskey colas in Kyiv, that Babay revealed more about the soldier.

"The military's story goes to say that he was shot by Separatists while he was backing up his brothers in arms while they were falling back. And the fucking bad thing about this story, and the thing that we didn't tell his parents or nobody, he was shot with the caliber of a Ukrainian weapon."

A friendly fire death. By then, it was something quite believable and realistic, considering the often-non-publicized chaos and disorganization of the volunteer movement that I was beginning to understand more with each interview.

"We do this for the family. If they knew the truth, they would be devastated," he explained to me much later, after the exhibit in Chicago and before the New York opening, when I again resurfaced the topic during a night of verbal exfoliation. Not only from the weeks and months of recording and internalizing the volunteers' stories, but from walking within the community and understanding the profound role that the nature of heroism continued to play in their lives.

How could they ever walk in the peace life with ease, in a world that couldn't understand their reality, when they were shackled against speaking the truth of it? When they were bound to perpetuate, whether by verbal repetition or remaining silent, inflated stories of heroism that surpassed reality, covered truths, and sometimes inadvertently created comparisons, minimizing the actions of those who were there, standing beside them?

Without an ending to the war, it seemed they would carry these burdens for years ... when the mothers of the fallen each year pleaded for the comrades of their lost sons and daughters to attend an annual memorial, which seemed like a repetition of the funeral. The procession to the cemetery, the flowers and the smoke of the Orthodox priest's blessing, the candles, the crying and prayers. The repetition of the reception, where stories would be told again and again, around a long dining table with raised glasses, toasts and tears. Stories that wouldn't allow the families of these soldiers to suffer an additional pain, but often stories that didn't reveal the full truth about war, only romanticized versions of fire and glory.

ALINA GORDEEVA

TRANSLATED EXCERPT FROM INTERVIEW
KYIV, UKRAINE, 2018

I don't know, any time I start thinking about that period, I think of my combat comrades who are already gone, more specifically one combat comrade. ... I remember how we made coffee in a cup using fuel tabs ... Yes, that I do recall quite often, how we were making coffee and looking at the whole town that is right in front of you. And down there, they were doing some drills at the time, maybe the tenth drill that day. They liked to do drills at the base. And then they liked everybody walking around and showing off so that the officers could be seen.

But ... I remember the guys. I don't have any negative memories. You start understanding that human life is so short; and the value of human life is probably what's most important and that all those problems with your job or being afraid of your boss, those are such trifles. And people focus on that so much without even understanding that they have something fundamental: their lives.

Silence of the Quarry Trench

In the silence of standing in a quarry trench, it's almost as if the air is gone, sucked into a white noise, even though I'm still breathing perfectly fine. It gives way to sounds that are often muted by the chaos of everyday life. Sounds carried from kilometers away. A military tarp blowing in the wind, dogs barking from a distant frontline village, the muffled voices of soldiers, boots crunching against broken rocks, the unbalanced planks of wood teetering under the weight of soldiers crossing over the mud puddles. Even the distant vibrations and blasts of artillery and the faint popping of gunfire are a comfort in this place.

We hiked through the Donbas mud after days of November rain to reach the positions at the top of the quarry mountains, moving along the caked-up mud that hugged the sunken tire tracks on a dirt road already warped by farming vehicles. Breathing, lungs, my weight tripled by the inches of quicksand earth mercilessly clinging to my feet. It was a reminder of how easy it was to fall into a kind of comfortable, the kind where one forgets that he or she may need to run to preserve life.

"So, where do you want to go?" Ira had asked me the previous day. Ira, the unofficial 93rd Brigade press officer, clearly ran the operations for her team. She was the only press officer I wasn't hesitant to work with over the years, beginning with the first time she picked me up at the train station in Volnovakha, which I realized was only in a metaphoric sense as she wheeled up on a bicycle. But she always found a way to support the ideas I was after, finding ways to circumvent or barrel through the rules and bureaucracy that often worked against them.

Her question was appropriate, because I normally had an

agenda for her, a longer form story to develop over multiple trips to the front line: the coexistence of farmers working the sunflower, corn and wheat fields adjacent to the soldiers in trenches; the reality of oligarchs and industry on both sides of the border dictating the schedule of artillery falling; the 2014 volunteers still serving on the front line, stuck in the "should I stay or should I go" mentality, or the transparency of where the billion-dollar US support packages to Ukraine were going, because they certainly weren't visible on the front line. Soldiers were still buying their own weapons, cars and often their own uniforms in lieu of the upgraded and newly designed pixels the Ministry of Defense proudly issued them, pretty for standing in a parade and in tatters a month later.

But a story wasn't my ambition that day. I didn't really have any ambitions past the need to escape the peace life in Kyiv, where even I began feeling detached from the reality of war, no matter the proximity. Soldiers continued to die each week. It felt as if it were happening in another world, another time, so far away and removed from my existence. Like when I left the Army, it was so easy to forget about it all. Once I was away from Afghanistan, from Iraq, and even before I left the service, the death counts just became death counts. Statistics and numbers without faces and stories.

Just a few more moments in the quarry trench, leaning against the wall, taking it all in. I let the other journalist, a reporter out of western Ukraine, walk far away through the maze of trenches to cover the soldiers manning the big guns, asking what they thought of the recent news, the escalation of troops again on the other side of the border; were they prepared and ready? Take your time, I'm content in this place without the rush and competition; as nice as he was, it felt as though he were an invading tourist.

Because the disconnect wasn't only about the war's reality. It was a disconnect from a place, from a world, from a people. Of real and raw and simplicity. Where no one knows what you're doing, where you are, except the people who are there with you. No external obligations back home, paperwork, bureaucracy, phones … only stay in the moment. Because there is nothing more important than that moment. Being in Kyiv too long became very much the way

Valera had explained it from the forest floor in Popasna. This focus on the trivial, being surrounded by a proclaimed attachment to an unshared experience, fighting and working against one another instead of focusing on those simplicities we find when working together to stay alive.

I revert to the bunker under the earth, the kitchen area, the sleeping quarters, the downtime caves. Back to where a puppy and two kittens stalk the chow table for handouts of government cheese and sausage slices, or if they're lucky, a prized piece of meat from unfinished borscht or soup. I photograph a white cat who pushes himself against the soldier resting and smoking a cigarette near the tarp opening. If any soldiers on the front line had disliked animals in their past, I found it hard to believe any of them could avoid conversion. They softened the hardest of spirits.

The unit cook emerges from the kitchen area and hands me a cup of tea, my hand burning while the plastic essentially molds to my skin under the heat. I rest it on the table to cool off and notice the young soldier who dodged our path earlier, running off to some faraway corner out of view. I watch him clean a rifle under a lamp light, methodically, a calming motion, and listen to the sounds of the metal rod pushing through the barrel.

"Can I take a few shots?'

He nods without looking, and somewhere in a frame, as his comrades play with him and throw banter over his shyness, I catch a smile.

He was dead the next day.

YEVHENIA YANCHENKO

EXCERPT FROM INTERVIEW
KYIV, UKRAINE, 2018

I want my country to live in peace. I want the kids going to school or daycare without worrying about missiles hitting the school or daycare.

Ninety-nine percent of the children always ask one question: When will this be finished? We say the truth. That we can't answer. Because we don't know.

MARION

MARION WAS THE FIRST OF THE FACES I had photographed who died on the front line. It happened only a few months after I met him in 2018, and not far from the fresh ditch in the ground where Dylan had contemplated how just a slight calibration from drone footage would finish any of them off on any given day.

He was the young man in the huddle of soldiers, the last soldiers we spoke with during our first visit to the positions with DaVinci. The soldier Dylan was referring to as we walked away, asking me in astonishment, "What is he doing here? He can't be more than eighteen."

Marion was a face I froze in time. Alive in the photograph, and it's as if I'm there, peering through the lens again when I look at it now. But then time becomes warped. I'm in two places at once, standing there in a moment when he was young and alive, but now wanting to look through the lens longer, to photograph him more before walking away. Because I understand what he doesn't—that in a short time, he will be merely a memory.

What would it take for the world to look through my lens? To understand that there was a war happening, that people, soldiers and civilians, were dying every week? What would it take for them to understand the irony and absurdity of it all, that over the years, as the war waged on and on, Russia wasn't noticed as a modern-day aggressor that invaded Ukraine in 2014, but rather as FIFA's nominated host for the 2018 World Cup. Or that while the EU and UN publicly condemned Russia's illegal annexation of Crimea and the invasion of the Donbas, the EU Human Rights Council nonetheless invited them to take a seat at the table. Or that Russia remained a permanent member of the UN Security Council, giving Putin and the Kremlin the power to make decisions regarding peace and war around the world, that they were actually considered peacekeepers in their own war against Ukraine, as if they weren't responsible for waging it? What would it take for them to understand that after the collapse of the Soviet Union, the United States and the United Kingdom persuaded Ukraine to surrender the world's third-largest nuclear arsenal to Russia. The 1994 Budapest Memorandum had given "assurances" that Russia would never attack Ukraine, that Russia would respect Ukraine's independence and territorial integrity. And that the US and UK would help ensure Russia obliged.

There was a message to be told, and I wanted the volunteers' voices to amplify this message and inspire the world, to show what it meant to fight for something real, for freedom, something America had lost along the way, when the Fourth of July had become a summer holiday of barbecues and fireworks and beer, empty of the inspiration of our Revolutionary War patriots. I wanted the volunteers' voices not just to be heard. I wanted them to be listened to, making it clear they were still there, still fighting for the same thing, still dying for the same cause, but in a war that fell back into the hands of the same system they wanted to escape, tangled in corruption and political endeavors. They were still there, fighting against an aggression that wouldn't stop at Ukraine's border.

The soldier who was cleaning weapons in the Novotroitske quarry trench in 2021, the one who shied away when I asked to take his photograph and was killed the following day, they called him Gera. The photographs I captured of him might be the last visual memory of his short lifetime. Just off the train in Kyiv, returning from my trip to his unit's positions in the Donbas, I hadn't even unpacked my ruck sack before reading the news. I immediately sent my photographs of him to Ira, long before uploading them to my photo agency for editorial coverage. She sent them to Gera's family.

It didn't feel like a coincidence, that Gera was killed in the very location where I had been, and the very next day. It felt more like a muscle flex from the other side, a slap in the face, a reminder that even I was subject to becoming a pawn in this war that had metastasized into a game.

American Patch

"I don't think anything will happen today," Ira had told me a few months before, during the summer, the first time I came to her in Hranitne to visit the positions where a logistics vehicle had been blown to pieces only a few days before. I'd just finished signing a waiver in the battalion's headquarters office, a new bureaucratic protocol, saying that I understood soldiers had just been killed there, that I accepted the risk that I might die in the same manner. In Ira's mind, signing this waiver wasn't something to cause a heightened sense of alarm; it was more like a notification of my arrival to the other side. In other words, nothing would happen before the lens of an American journalist. No illegal attacks on Ukrainian territory, no blood, nothing tangible or raw and real and visceral to sharpen the public's focus on the reality of the war or hold a politician to a standard. Much like the reality of no artillery attacks during the weeks of harvest in the Donbas, there would be nothing more than rear shots of soldiers walking through trenches or shots of soldiers drinking coffee and smoking cigarettes in the break tent.

It was a new system, unlike how it was in 2018 and 2019, the days when I could take a taxi right up to the front line in Popasna to see Valera. Everything had fallen under a web of policies, confined under a new title of the war; the Anti-Terrorist Operation was now officially titled the Joint Field Operation. Titles and semantics, leaflets in the sky, a reminder of when Bush, after no weapons of mass destruction were found in Iraq, renamed Operation Enduring Freedom to Operation Iraqi Freedom, as if the United States government gave a damn about saving the Iraqi people.

"Do I have to send my route to the press office?" I had asked

Ira a few weeks before arriving on a second visit to the area, a plead to bypass the protocols. Because I no longer felt safe in the entanglement of waivers, permission requests and the required detailed itineraries submitted to the press office before each frontline visit: dates, locations, units to visit, plate numbers, names of the driver and others in tow. I preferred staying off the grid and out of range of the government entities removed from the ground; out of range of the bargains and oligarchs and profiteering and information leaks, out of range of a system that worked against the very reason I was there: to tell the truth.

I don't think anything will happen today.

Her comment only solidified a distrust that stemmed from an event the previous year, in 2020. When I was driving through Zaitsevo in eastern Ukraine with Babay, sitting in the passenger seat of a local resident's car. He offered to take us to his home in the "gray" zone, less than 100 meters from where his wife once easily ventured to see her mother in the same neighborhood, before it was divided between Ukrainian territory and occupied territory.

"You look familiar. I've seen you somewhere," Babay translated from the back seat after the man glanced in my direction a few times, attempting to get a better look at my face as he drove.

"Maybe he recognized you from the news?" Babay joked. But it was only a joke in the sense that we both knew it was more than likely true, long before the man confirmed it. That yes, he'd seen me on the news. Some fantastic propaganda story rooted in the self-proclaimed Luhansk People's Republic, airing not only all over the internet but wired into televisions across eastern Ukraine.

"Tell him it's bullshit, please," I said. Honestly, I wasn't so sure if the man believed me or not.

The irony of it—while trying to fight the propaganda of politics and media, I had become a direct target of it. The details—my location, the date, vehicle plate number, and even the driver's name— were sent confidentially to the press center.

"Have you seen this?" I asked Vlad, who was serving as my press officer for the last day of my trip in Ira's absence. I handed him my phone from the front seat of the van as he bounced around in the row behind. As we returned from the positions near Hranitne, cell reception finally restored, I was receiving the latest headlines of Russia's new troop escalation, along with text messages from across the globe, telling me to get out of there.

He laughed in response to the latest reality distortion, a counter to Zelensky's public statement the previous day that Russia would attack within the next two days. This one was a quoted statement from a Russian politician, saying that Ukrainian troops were mobilizing and massing on their front lines in preparation to invade Russia.

"It's bullshit."

Of course. We were both there. It was business as usual on the front line, no imminent feeling of a full-scale Russian attack, no extra troops, no feeling of war in the air like in 2018, that rush and anticipation to fight and retake their land. But most amazing was my understanding that this was truly the dominant source of journalism given to the English-speaking world, republished and often distorted statements from politicians and presidents on mainstream networks that had the power to manipulate and even instigate the fictions they were painting into reality.

Vlad accompanied me back to the train station in Volnovakha that day, after we survived the predicted full-scale invasion. Ira was still out with another journalist, leaving me prey to the dreaded obsessive America inquisition. It was always a balancing act with Vlad, of how much I could take in one day, and if it weren't such a long haul on foot to the train platform in Volnovakha, loaded down with body armor, bags and camera equipment, I would have been content escorting myself alone that time.

"You were an officer in the American Army." He somehow managed to squeeze these words into any conversation, even if it made absolutely no sense in the scheme of discussion. And no matter how many times I tried talk down his respect, to cool it off, to explain that I'm not special just because I wore the American uniform, and certainly not special because I was an officer, or that the United States, America, is not exactly what it seems, my words just flew over him, under him or through one ear and out the other.

"But you're an American Army veteran!"

In the beginning it was easy—signing American flags, giving the American flag patch to soldiers on the front line. It was inspiring to accept the blind respect and eagerness to receive an olive drab and black piece of woven stripes and stars with Velcro. Maybe because I wanted America to represent everything they imagined. But over time, the longer I covered the war, the more I became acquainted with Ukraine's complex history, the more I realized how integrated my past was with Ukraine's struggle for independence, it faded into realism, and then almost guilt.

"You went to Afghanistan. To Iraq."

I would never take those days back. They forever shaped who I became, but at the same time, I wasn't sure if they realized that this sentiment, this collective experience of war, was perhaps the stronger connection between us, and not just a blind respect of the stars and stripes and the American uniform. Because my decision to be standing there with them, my decision to join their war, it was my decision this time, not America's.

ZHORA TURCHAK

TRANSLATED EXCERPT FROM INTERVIEW
KYIV, UKRAINE, 2018

*Fine! I will tell you. You bugged the fuck out of me with those
questions about when things changed. The first story:*

*When we entered Stepanivka, we could only advance
halfway ... So, we entered a school building. We got all the
wounded and the killed and we put them into different
classrooms. I was guarding the classroom with Separatists.
There were a few people who stood out in this group. I got into
a conversation with one of them. He was a Russian officer. Not
currently enlisted. He was discharged prior to the war. I was
just helping him not to croak before the morning comes, so he
can make it to the hospital, so we could keep it a little fucking
human. We started talking about nothing in particular. He came
two days before he was wounded. It was his first battle. And I
say, "Why the fuck did you come to my country, asshole?" He
said, "Because I watched TV, they said there were women and
children being killed by the fascists in Ukraine." So, he says he
got to Stepanivka yesterday and saw children walking around,
moms with strollers. He says, "Had you not come yesterday, I
would have left Ukraine." And I understood that he was sincere
because he knew he was going to die. He asked me to write a
letter to his mom detailing where he died and how he died. So, I
wrote a letter to his mom and sent it.*

MESSAGE IN A BOTTLE

JANUARY 2022
KYIV, UKRAINE

Babay was there at the Chicago opening, standing next to me when the guest pointed out the photograph of the memorial plaque and thanked me. We immediately looked at each other; a moment of understanding between us, but for me, it was an additional moment of guilt. Guilt in becoming a part of the silence. Not only about the possible nature of the memorialized soldier's death, but about the nature of heroism.

During the US exhibits in 2019 and 2020, it was easier to dismiss, easier to avoid constantly correcting and clarifying that my project wasn't a celebration of heroism. But then it began to spiral out of control, infiltrating the nature of my message and my project, almost as if it were using it as a vesicle to spread within the Ukrainian community, a rebranding of the word "revolutionaries" to "Ukraine's heroes." The people gathered around the portraits in an exhibit space didn't hear their voices, the one- to four-hour audio stories that weren't about heroism, at least not self-proclaimed heroism. Heroism, when mentioned, wasn't described with pride, but in the way I often captured their photos in the peace life, in moments of darkness, depression and isolation with a bottle in hand, at memorials while choosing the right words to comfort mothers and fathers of lost comrades, in turn reliving moments in their minds that they'd rather avoid, or even in photos of celebrations and reunions void of the civil society, joking over the newest piece of cheap and already tarnished metal chucked to the side after the ceremony, or satire over the most recent scumbag receiving the highest of honors. It was described in the way that all soldiers experience the nature of heroism when heroism is branded by those removed from the experience.

When the opportunity to exhibit in Kyiv first presented itself, I imagined it would help burn through the false perceptions of soldiers and veterans often created by political agendas and media in a country at war. That it would be an opportunity to narrow the divide of understanding between those who only understood the peace life and those in the soldier-veteran community. And now we finally had the addition of sound, how I always envisioned the work to be shown. Not just as portraits and text excerpts on a wall, but portraits in a room where the subjects' voices resonated throughout the space. But as the opening date approached, as the marketing of "heroes" pressed even deeper, no matter how many times I tried to correct it, the more I feared an absolute disaster approaching, that it was an ultimate betrayal. Not only a betrayal to the community, but to myself, that by letting it move forward, I was inadvertently promoting heroism as a core message when it was a concept that I wanted to shred and burn. Knowing that I might inadvertently downplay the significance of others, the hundreds and thousands I had never had a chance to interview. Knowing that some were already arguing, judging each other, comparing a status of heroism, refusing to hang next to each other on a wall because of peace-life problems and medal counts, forgetting the ultimate reason they were hanging together in the first place. Something that went back to a time when they didn't care about press or heroism. A time when their purpose wasn't tangled under the government and run by a system of achievements and medals and plaques and propaganda that satiated and manipulated the public, allowing a war that should have ended years ago to continue without change. A system that silenced a purpose they felt together so strongly in 2014, and now it was slowly pushing them away from one another.

In December 2021, only three months from the scheduled Kyiv opening, I'm sitting in a cafe outside the front-line town of Hranitne for a break of chicken bouillon and warmth. The photo story I'm working on, about the industrial mines, quarries and oligarchs influencing the war's outcome, has been abruptly snowed out and then snubbed out by a 15:45 winter sunset. A large and entirely out-of-place flat-screen television, probably provided through war funding packages and American aid to support "Ukraine's sovereignty," hangs on the wall, a comfort gesture often seen when making wars more permanent and attractive to new sign-ups and renewed contracts. A group of soldiers sit at a table nearby, their plates and cups empty, checks paid. As they stand to put on their coats, scarves and hats before heading back to their positions on the front, they linger for a few extra moments, tuning into a story on the national news. I turn around to look at the television and see a familiar face: Da Vinci, the Right Sector volunteer soldier, the one who had no interest in politics and government, smiling cheek to cheek while shaking hands with President Zelensky as he receives a Hero of Ukraine award, the highest award that can be given to an individual citizen by the president of Ukraine.

Three weeks later, I see Da Vinci again in the public spotlight, this time with two other 2014 volunteers I worked with in 2018, sitting at a formal dinner table with the president, politicians, oligarchs, champagne glasses and suits and ties and gowns. It's Ukraine's annual presidential New Year's toast, a drawn-out election advertisement. And as the hours pass into night on social media, images of the event are accompanied by an accumulating wave of hypocrisy callouts from angry soldiers and veterans, plenty of whom they once served with, including Valkyrie.

The idea of canceling the exhibit altogether wasn't moving on and away without serious contemplation. The only other solution I had, and one that I knew would not fly over easily, was to remove their names and bios from the wall. To hang blankets over their portraits and obscure the faces they knew and recognized, and just let the audio echo off the walls of the institute. Because maybe if they listened to one another's stories, they would be reminded that they share a human experience that has changed them forever.

Dreaming Is Easy

Highway 144. The final twenty-two-mile stretch of narrow two-way highway, a tunnel through a sea of towering Georgia pine that perfectly framed a full moon on the drive in for morning PT. It was a blackout highway, no lights, no cell reception to call in and let the commander know you were running late, and no pit stops between the back gate of Fort Stewart and the gas station at the opposite end, at the I-95 exit.

Lieutenant Goldstein and I had many idiotic races down this highway on the drive home to Savannah after work, leaving base and rolling the dice with the MPs—one mile over forty was all it took, a little private first class having a field day writing up an officer, a ticket that would get reported right back to the battalion commander in addition to a monetary fine. But I didn't care—this was life, the hour of freedom, heading back home, driving those forty-five minutes to a non-military world, a world where I could ditch the uniform at the end of the day and forget that the government owned me.

It was a route I knew well: twenty-two miles east on 144, then picking up 95-N, four lanes of catch-up and pass opportunity if Goldstein took the lead before the official end of the race, exiting onto Highway 204, the Southside of Savannah, where I'd drive north past her apartment complex and turn right onto King George Boulevard to mine, right across the street from the twenty-four-hour Waffle House, a place I'd frequent after "weekend warrior" nights downtown with people completely unrelated to the military. Goldstein and I had our own agendas on the weekends, and more than enough hours logged together at base during the work week.

I met her in November 2000, when I was new to the company and terrified of walking into my first job in the regular Army as a platoon leader. But the apprehension quickly dissipated and a friendship evolved, first over a little bit of crass and sharp "get over it" mentorship, followed by bumming hundreds of cigarettes from each other, taking turns bringing in Burger King or Combos and machine cappuccinos from the PX for breakfast, teaming up to prank our platoon sergeants and cracking far too many jokes at others' misfortune (including each other's). We had a nickname for everyone, and we both shared the sentiment that an extra thirty minutes of sleep was not a good enough reason to live in Hinesville, the town adjacent to Fort Stewart, and what I considered to be the standard military town, the kind of place created as a by-product of the base it catered to, full of chains, fast food restaurants, tattoo parlors, barber shops, liquor stores, strip joints, video rental shops. It was the stereotype of an Army soldier's needs.

Savannah was entirely different. Even though it was host to Hunter Army Airfield, a smaller Army base where I wished I could have been stationed, the city had been there long before, since 1733 to be exact. And Highway 204, right outside my apartment complex, was a direct shot to the heart of its downtown squares, an eclectic city of mysterious southern locals, fishermen, and art students from the Savannah College of Art and Design. I could get lost there, walking among the coffee shops and pubs and people and everything normal and non-military, everything that kept me connected to the world where I belonged that was only four years from my reach.

Before returning from Afghanistan, we decided to ditch our apartments on the Southside of Savannah and room together downtown, somewhere right off Forsyth Park. Why live halfway to freedom? Sacrificing an additional twenty minutes of sleep was well worth the cost.

The races got even better. Now passing the 204 exit and picking up I-16 off I-95, we had thirteen additional interstate miles of speeding and passing opportunity before reaching an array of strategic options at the downtown street exits. Take Gwinnett Street and risk a red at the traffic light? Wait it out for a straight shot across MLK Boulevard, or take a right on red and risk an indefinite pause to northbound traffic taking a left to cross? Recklessly weaving through the small city streets, we finally had a concrete finish line: the first one to pull into the little parking lot across from the house we rented on Waldburg Street.

We kept the house when we left for Iraq the next year, deciding it was worth the cost to have a furnished home waiting for our arrival rather than storing all our belongings and wasting time searching for a new apartment on returning. But once the lease neared its end the second time around, shortly after we came back from Iraq, we knew it was time to move on. Because Goldstein was nearing the end of her contract. She was gone by the end of 2003. And gone with her were the dreams of going into business together in the free world.

We'd talked about it plenty during our downtime, on base at Fort Stewart, or when we were throwing rocks into tin cans in Afghanistan and Iraq. One of our favored options was to open a bar—maybe in Savannah, maybe in New York. And we'd do more than just own it. We'd be a part of its daily life, bartending and mingling with the patrons, playing our own music every now and then. Because she dreamed of becoming a DJ one day, maybe in New York or London, and I still dreamed of becoming a rock star, secondary to writing a book that would change the world.

Dreaming is easy when you're still serving, when you're still counting down the days. The future is wide open, the possibilities endless. And then the day comes. Terminal leave, a maximum of two months paid vacation if you strategically saved up your time. Freedom. And then a sudden realization that you still haven't figured out what you want to be when you grow up. Even if you had some ideas, some dreams, how do you get there now, this many years later in life? And for the first time in years, you realize there's no one telling you what to do. There's no one telling you where to be. You spent years of your life without having to consider tomorrow or the next week or the next month or the next year. You didn't have to think about what to do next; you simply had to do as you were told. And then as the years pass, you realize that no matter what you do, no matter what dream you pursue, nothing measures up to the sense of purpose you felt when you were in the war zone.

When you were responsible for your soldiers, your comrades, when life and death were on the line, when getting each other home was on the line.

Dreaming is easy when you're still counting down the days. And I was always counting down the days. Counting down the days until Beast summer training was over, or the days until we'd be recognized cadets and would no longer have to ping back and forth between classes and memorize trivia for the upperclassmen's entertainment in the mess hall. I was counting down the days until graduation, until we'd leave Afghanistan and then Iraq, and even in the back of my calendar, where there's a five-year projection in tiny month clusters, I had a date circled—the final day I was counting down to—when I'd be out of the military and free of the government's tendrils forever. I was always counting down to this place where I thought the present would be all that I needed, where I'd be in the world where I belonged, as a civilian, living a life of freedom to pursue my dreams. But even when I was counting down the days, there was always this voice in the back of my head, in Afghanistan, in Iraq, even at West Point, reminding me that I was going to miss it one day. Not exactly the place, but what the place gave us, and what it created between us. I just didn't realize how much I missed it until I first stepped foot inside Ukraine.

KILL LIST

February 23, 2022
Kyiv, Ukraine

"Do you really think something's going to happen this time?" I asked Misha the previous month.

Misha, Aidar callsign "Chechnya," wasn't the type to just throw words into the air without solid confidence, so I took the weeks of his foreboding responses quite seriously, responses to any statement or question that alluded to planning after January.

After the war.

Let's wait until we see the dead bodies of our enemies flowing down the river.

Always pacing back and forth in thought, hands clasped behind his back, Misha was often mentally fact-checking his words before reigniting a conversation that all others assumed was finished. Evenings in his presence routinely manifested into an atmosphere filled with political, historic, or cultural lectures followed by debates, and if there was ever a shred of uncertainty in an opposing opinion or a question left unanswered when he walked out the door, he always came back later. Sometimes the same evening, sometimes after weeks or even months, to follow up with new supporting evidence to ensure his words were appreciated, valued, and trusted.

Rock solid serious, never smiling, always giving the knuckle-bump greeting if he sensed an attempted embrace, Misha's presence was easily intimidating and overpowering for someone who hadn't invested time to understand the other side of him: a sci-fi writer, poet, and philosopher of monkish tranquility behind closed doors. I respected him and our discussions, even when butting heads over his insistence that every Ukrainian who hadn't yet learned the language was a shame to their culture. Because Misha

93

not only ensured every question posed to him was answered thoroughly, even if it seemed far below his intelligence level, he also took the time to ask questions. He was thirsty for and eager to share knowledge, to educate those from the West about the centuries of complex history that shaped the future in a land, a culture and a part of the world I was beginning to call my home.

It will happen from the north, Belarus. Kyiv will be the target.
When?

After the Olympics.

I didn't need Russian fluency to conceptualize Putin's words on February 21, the day after the Olympics ended. Or to understand the clear intention in between his words, of what was to come next. It was all there, in his voice, in his eyes, in his posture, this demented narcissism and egotistical confidence, a tone and rhythm of conclusion, authority and undebatable decisiveness, taking me right back to my apartment in Savannah that evening in October 2001, when President Bush declared his war on terrorism.

Eight years of peace agreements and diplomacy went out the window with Putin's signature. It was as if he finally removed the mask of bureaucratic protection to the entire world, blowing all the stock photos of political handshakes and video conference meetings and signing treaties into the wind. He didn't need to pretend anymore. He'd already won this game he'd been scheming for decades, testing the waters here, testing the waters there, patient and piece by piece, using a system of diplomacy that was intended to prevent the worst in the world to aid him in doing exactly the opposite.

"I need to go back to Poland to pick up Miroslava. They can't watch her anymore," Valkyrie said.

My jaw dropped. Surely, they could keep her a little longer. Didn't they understand? The Olympics were over. Putin just recognized the Luhansk People's Republic and Donetsk People's Republic as sovereign nations and mobilized his troops on a "peacekeeping" mission into their territories along Ukraine's border, the same territories he occupied illegally in 2014. The entire staff of the US Embassy had hightailed it out of Lviv in western Ukraine, where they had first relocated, to across the border in Poland, or in other words, every single American government employee had cleared out of the country. And now Valkyrie, who had taken her daughter to her godmother's house in Warsaw only a few days prior, a planned two-week safety measure to wait out the risk, was bringing her daughter back into Ukraine on the very brink of war.

"Where should we go? Maybe just come back to Kyiv?" Valkyrie wrote before boarding the return flight from Warsaw to Lviv.

"No! Please, don't bring her back here," I responded.

Not Kyiv. Not with a child. Not when Valkyrie's name had already been added to multiple Russian kill lists over the years. Not when the possibility of a ground attack, in addition to air strikes, was a clear reality, foot soldiers and tanks in neighborhood streets. The Russian troops were also massed at the border of Belarus, only 200 kilometers north.

My advice should have felt rational enough, but I somehow still questioned myself, whether my concern was solid or simply redirected Westernized pressure. Because Valkyrie's daughter was the only child missing from the ranks of school; it went on as routine without a single peep or mention of war or an emergency plan discussed; only "flowers or cookies?" for teachers' gifts and fees for dance class filled the parents' chat group. Ukraine's primary dialogue from their side was simply, "Don't panic."

"J.T., are you out of there yet?" my photo editor wrote.

His email arrived just moments after I finished sending off a response to the organizers of the Kyiv exhibit, confirming that yes, I was still there in Kyiv and had every intent to follow through with the opening.

"It's not worth it," he added, reminding me that not only was I a former target of Russian propaganda in 2020, but that I was also an American journalist and American combat veteran, which he equated to the perfect resume for qualification on Russia's "denazifying" Ukraine kill list. And he also knew the game of journalism, how once upon a time important stories were told before the days of sensationalizing and mass exploitation. I had already tried to tell the once-upon-a-time type of story, but it seemed as if no one was listening. And now the world of media swarmed throughout the country like a pack of hyenas, targeting many of the volunteers in my project for interviews and stories to make headlines, hounding me for connections, and even going so far as targeting myself for an interview, this American who was still Ukraine.

"Are you coming?" Valkyrie wrote to me from a bus en route to Ozliiv from Lviv, the only place where I could help to find backup lodging west of Kyiv.

I looked at my dog, Cuba, who slept lazily on the couch next to me. There was no way I was risking the last months or years of his life to be spent under bombs, or to become the accomplice pet of an American journalist on a Russian kill list. I could at least take him west, evaluate and regroup my thoughts and the situation.

"I'm sorry," I told him, knowing his sixteen-year-old ears couldn't hear me anymore.

"Packing up and leaving soon," I responded.

ALINA VIATKINA

EXCERPT FROM INTERVIEW
KYIV, UKRAINE, 2018

The war is not finished in Ukraine. So, every day I'm thinking: What will be if Russia will go further? What will be if Russia will go to Kyiv?

And when I'm talking about these things, I feel a lot of fear because I'm not sure it can be in real life. All these things like nuclear weapons and Russian tanks in Kyiv. But we never thought that Russian tanks can be in Donetsk before it happened.

I have this backpack, which is always standing ready to go. I have my medicine here and documents and clothes ... uniform, of course. So when I am talking to my mother about it, she is just laughing. But I think it's something we need to do while the war is going on. People forget that it's happening because they're not there.

I remember when Russia started to occupy Crimea. It was such a shock for Ukraine, for everyone. And I remember people from the west, east, north and from the south tried to move to Kyiv or to any other part of country just to go further from Crimea because everyone was so scared. Nobody knows what will they do next. What will be the next step of Russia? And I'm not sure we need to be so relaxed about it.

OZLIIV

FEBRUARY 24, 2022
OZLIIV, UKRAINE

A morning in Ozliiv, the only place I was able to find lodging on such short notice. Seems like everyone has already moved as far west as possible.

It's so quiet in the winter here. Just birds chirping and my dog sniffing grass. No traffic on this isolated road, no people.

There's a lake in the distance. I imagine I'd like it here in the summer, swimming and fishing, shashlik, and that I'll come back again when the seasons turn. I also imagine that I would have heard the explosions this morning, that they should have woken me, that the sounds would have carried all the way over the terrain and through the silence from Kyiv, from Ivano-Frankivsk, from Lutsk, a city only forty kilometers away. From all of the places in Ukraine where metal dropped from sky to earth, this same sky that was open to commercial airline traffic only yesterday. But the only sounds of this come from my mobile phone, from posted videos, from social media channels, from a little speaker on an electronic device, and now they are dominating this space. They are filling the space.

~

I regretted the decision even in the moment of making it, because Ozliiv, some random village south of Rivne and nowhere near Kyiv, felt safe enough, and it should have been enough to calm my family. But it's almost as if I didn't make the decision, as if I wasn't there inside of my own being, only a spectator looking on from some alternate dimension. I see our bags moving back and forth, being loaded into the car and then unloaded, moving with our indecisiveness to stay or leave, to stay or leave. I see days' worth of new groceries sitting in the refrigerator and on the counter and dishes unwashed, as if we didn't realize ourselves that we were leaving, as if we intended to turn back around. I see my dog moving about like a zombie, still coming off the anxiety drugs that I gave him for the drive from Kyiv, trying to establish a sense of place, the ground underneath his feet, to understand why I yanked him from his home, again, only to leave again. I see the summer-warped roads and police officers pulling us over at checkpoints, searching for men of conscription age who might be on the run.

Ozliiv should have been enough. Because we didn't even plan to leave Kyiv. We'd gone back and forth about it for days and even weeks, each hoping the other had the right answer, the solution, each of us battling the reality that we had responsibilities outside of our own bodies and beings, because if something was about to happen, in Ukraine, in Kyiv, then that's where we were both meant to be. Valkyrie not only as a soldier, but as a new citizen of Ukraine, ready to fight again alongside her comrades, her friends, to defend her homeland with the people who embraced her so many years ago, to fight for the people she lost so many years ago. And for myself, to be a voice from the inside, to tell a story from the ground as one of them, connected and standing there alongside, a different voice among the mainstream media headlines.

We were ready to make it work; Valkyrie's daughter was supposed to be safe in Poland, I had a go-bag and a rental car on standby if things went south, we scrounged up some of the last available Kevlar and body armor from a ballistics shop in Kyiv.

Ozliiv should have been enough. It was enough for me to stay and feel out the situation. It was my own decision to be there, measured and thought out and not influenced by the pressures of a disconnected Western world I no longer identified with. The months on end of media headlines, an invasion "within days" from President Biden, the US Embassy's warnings for US citizens to evacuate immediately, the panic from my family on the other side of the world, it was all enough to make my head spin, but none of it was enough to make me panic, to make me just up and leave all of Ukraine.

You're all I have, Jenn, please.

My mom's tears ran through the phone and into my ears before stabbing somewhere inside. It was the first time I ever heard her cry.

Ozliiv should have been enough. And I resented it all. For caving into the pressure, for putting my dog through even more stress, for sitting in that fucking car for forty hours, watching my city burn, listening to friends panic, friends crying, friends sheltering in bunkers, friends, civilians, who should never have to experience this kind of trauma of war.

The exhaust, the dust, the dirt, every inch we moved forward to reach that godforsaken border, every pant of my dog, every text message from faraway family asking if we were there yet—each one was just another minute of added resentment, of anger, of guilt. But how would they ever understand more than what they were watching on television? How would they ever understand what it was like to live in a country eternally on the edge of invasion? How would they ever understand that this felt as if I were abandoning my own country, my own people, my own tribe?

STALIN

BEFORE WE LEFT FOR AFGHANISTAN, and even during my years at West Point, I often thought about America's history in war. Was there a war that I believed in, that may have achieved a higher purpose that made it worth its tragic aftermath? I needed to justify whether it was fair that I joined the military, knowing the possibility that I might be commanded to serve in a war, that I signed a contract to obey commands, that I might be ordered to kill faceless enemies on their own land, or that I'd be faced with the decision to kill to protect my own life.

Vietnam always took the forefront image, needless death and pain, corruption, the slaughtering of so many innocent people, and it was the veterans who took the brunt of the blame on returning home. Many were brutalized by a civilian population, paying the price for our leaders' mistakes, for doing what they were told, for blindly believing or obeying in fear of reprisal. But World War II was the wild card, the one possible "good" war, because it carried this illusion of heroism and saving innocent lives from an evil, genocidal maniac.

When I realized I might have a project interest in Ukraine, when I knew I was traveling to a land I knew nothing about, I read, I asked questions, I cursed myself for the spec and dump style of studying that had carried me through military history courses at West Point. But even if I had paid attention, if I had saved my old textbooks, I'm not sure I'd come close to understanding what I understand now. Because often the lessons of history only tell a story of what our institutions want us to remember. Propaganda is not reserved for Russia, though Russia may have mastered it.

I'm not surprised that to this day, there's still not a Holodomor Museum in Washington, DC. Because that might break the illusion of World War II in American history. It might put a bold font on the grayed-over parts of the story: how the United States government turned a blind eye to Stalin's man-made famine that killed millions of Ukrainians from 1932 to 1933.

It was a reign of terror no less brutal than Hitler's, and one that many historians believe far surpassed Hitler's. Instead of holding that evil to the fire, instead of acknowledging the cries for help that finally broke through Stalin's tightly silenced system in a state-sponsored genocide, we allied with him. We memorialized the millions who tragically died by the Nazis while burying the memory of the millions who perished under our government's lesser evil at the time.

Ukraine remembers. Or rather, the Ukrainian people remember. It's in their blood, passed on from a generation of survivors, some who still cannot bear to speak the stories, to relive the horrors. Despite all of this, the Ukrainian people still seem to have an unwavering trust in the United States, that America would protect them from the next wave of evil. Even after Crimea and the 2014 invasion. Even after February 24, 2022.

"I'll be okay. America won't let this happen," a friend had written to me from his homemade bunker in Kyiv, taking shelter from the air sirens as Valkyrie and I sat in the evacuation line to Poland, watching the invasion unfold from our phones in horror, listening to testimonies from friends as they felt the heat of the fire in real time. I was trying to urge him, to urge all I knew outside of the fight-again community, to go anywhere west and further from the city, away from the columns of Russian tanks that were staying on course to Kyiv. And I also knew what he wasn't ready to believe: that America could let this happen. That they were able to stand and watch the relentless bombings of apartment buildings, residential villages, shopping malls, schools, and restaurants, that they could allow the Russian tanks to continue on course and make it all the way into Kyiv without making the kind of decision that most all in Ukraine hoped for and imagined. Something decisive and serious, something that would put an end to it quickly, not simply sanctions, public condemnations and promises of equipment and aid packages that I already knew would take far too much time to make a difference in the present, and that's even if it made it into the right hands. And there was nothing I could do about any of it.

"They need radios!" Valkyrie screamed through her tears.

She knew she couldn't be a soldier, not in that moment. And what story was there left for me to tell as a photojournalist? There was no photograph I could take to change the horror that was already in motion, and if there was, there were plenty of journalists on the ground to capture it. But we could get those radios.

Russian Tanks in Kyiv

Four years earlier, Alina Viatkina had sat across from me in a flat, almost mocking herself for painting a surreal vision that had just become a reality: there were Russian tanks in Kyiv. But even then, she recognized that her insecurity of sounding excessive or paranoid may have simply been influenced by too much separation from her experience in 2014, from the war. She knew that many of the volunteers had lost touch, especially those who left the front line and tried to move on in the peace life, where it was so easy to forget. And those who stayed on the front line, tangled with the young privates disconnected from 2014 who joined for the big paychecks and benefits, they too felt an experience and community drifting away.

Even I struggled to remember the entirety of the emotion surrounding 9/11. It was there in memory, but as visions and facts in my brain, often absent of the once-attached emotions that fell from my pen and into the pages of my journal. The uncertainty of what was to follow, of standing on an earth spinning out of control, a version of myself closing, the version who only comprehended a world where the worst of evil was far away and removed to another place in another time. But it came back to me on February 24, 2022. And it stayed with me.

"Do you remember how random Iraq was?" Dylan had said that night four years ago in Kostyantynivka. And yes, I had remembered it, but just as with 9/11, not in its entirety. Until now.

Because now I move in and out of a world where I'm constantly reminded that in a flash, anything can change, when that distant universe of impossible collides with the present for a moment. When routinely driving east on the E373 from Kovel, from the Zosin-Ustyluh border to Kyiv, or on the H22 to Rivne, passing through the same towns where a familiar gas station, restaurant or hotel off the main road that was functioning two weeks ago is now a mound of war debris. Or when walking to a shopping center, the sound of flight overhead is no longer a background sound of normalcy, or the sight of movement in the sky, a jet flashing in and out in the peripheral vision, only long enough to *think* you saw something. It's that intersection, a pause in a space of white noise, bracing for blackness to follow, like that day in the streets of Nasiriyah, the man in the store, the crowds cheering. But then it's over. The sound of explosions in the distance, flashes illuminating the night clouds of a cityscape from a high rise flat, smoke rising from a burning structure or a field in the distance, or war manufactured, smoke rings and streaks in the sky, it confirms it's not right here, this wave is over, so we move about our day, our mission. Because we have a mission, and it's our own mission.

Tourniquets, medical aid, secure radios, night vision thermals, rangefinders, chemical masks, boots and uniforms, we're putting them into the hands of the right people, the people we've known and trusted, who are fighting the invasion nearly empty-handed. We're collecting them in Poland from an international community that helps us fight the bureaucracy of international taxes and laws and regulations. They're flying them personally in hand luggage from the United States, from Sweden. They're sending us money without caring about tax-free donation receipts so that we can buy locally, even from the dreaded war profiteers if no other option is fast enough. Because they know this is our home. And they know that we'll take those supplies home: we'll take them to our people.

We're a small operation, but we're not mandated or confined to the bureaucracy of the United States, Ukraine, Poland, the EU, NATO, or the giant NGO monsters collecting billions of dollars. We're not stuck in the red tape of signed memorandums or the policy forbidding all government-employed Americans to cross the border into Ukraine in fear of Russian reprisal and being sucked into World War III. Because it already is World War III, and we're not waiting for thousands to die if we can help even one.

So, we wait in line at that fucking border between Ukraine and Poland, again and again and again, sometimes for five hours, sometimes for twenty hours, driving back and forth from Poland to Ukraine. We just drive to where we're needed and adjust to the changing landscape of a peace life battlefield. One day in Rivne, one day in Kharkiv, on to Odessa, the next day in Kyiv, and on to gather more supplies. We just drive without understanding if the home we call home is a physical place or a state of mind. It doesn't matter. We just drive.

Maidan and then Crimea, the insurgency into eastern Ukraine in 2014, 9/11, these events were once the connection point between me and the revolutionaries, the experience of an intersection, when the impossible becomes possible, woven tightly around second thread, the experience of war. But February 24 connected us in a new way, because this time, we experienced it together. And we'd fight it together.

Valera Boldyrev

Translated Excerpt from Interview
Kyiv, Ukraine, 2019

As a kid I saw what war is. I clearly remember how my mom was carrying me, I was still very young, and there was a GAZ-66 truck passing with dismembered bodies lying on top of it. They were just piled up, in a stash. Even back then I realized that I will never in my life allow the people, that part of the society that I consider my nation, my country, I won't let them see this hell. Because it kills you with no bullets, no weapons, just the way it killed me.

I will stop when my comrades won't be dying anymore, when they will stop killing off my nation, when we will be left alone, when we will start developing normally, when these bastards will get the fuck out of here. I won't fight anymore. I won't even go hunting. I may even leave the gun shop and sell all my weapons. Maybe then I will even start doing something. I don't know, I don't want to plan ahead.

I have been to the States, I have been to Europe, I have seen how people live there. Specifically—live. And they get to be living, not just surviving. I won't put my weapons in a closet, I won't take off my uniforms until that day comes. I realize quite well that we won't see it in my lifetime.

It's Just Meat

"Do you wanna see some dead Russians?" Max asked from the driver's seat, cutting a brief glance my way to measure the shock value of my reaction.

"Why not?" I replied, hypnotized by the view through the side window, the skeleton of a lone gas station, blackened and burnt by war, the glaring overcast sky shining through the void of its lost muscle and flesh, sending it somewhere back in time, or maybe somewhere in the future. Something like Kandahar in early 2002, a collision of worlds when there is no era. Because it's all the same era, some cycle of war.

He chuckled at my response, which, honestly, even I was surprised by. Not only for my blasé, unfazed and empty tone, but for answering yes without some sort of extra comment, knowing that their offering was more an invitation to celebrate an iconic image of "fuck the Russians," rather than an offering of unbiased, journalistic value. But there was just nothing left in me, nothing left to feel, nothing left to understand in this world gone mad, in the death and loss, in the unfairness of it all, in the death of my dog, the one thing I thought I was protecting by crossing the border into Poland that first time.

"It's just meat," Lena explained from the cafeteria-style table seat next to me later that evening, after finishing a short celebration of Max's birthday with his Special Forces comrades in a school converted to a base camp in eastern Kharkiv. A school formerly attended by a demographic of children who sometimes returned to their former playground to proudly inform the soldiers, "My daddy is fighting on the other side."

She didn't understand why I wouldn't publish the photograph

108

she and Anya had asked me to take of them, posing with big smiles and thumbs-ups on both sides of a corpse that was so burnt that the odor of death had left him, splayed on a checkpoint barricade cross with his arms out, as if offering himself to a sun that had already sucked his soul. It was obvious he had been moved there, away from a cluster of corpses scattered on the ground near the remains of a gas station, their limbs twisted into unnatural positions not possible in living form, like tortured toy dolls that no longer interested the child torturing them.

"I have no anger anymore," she continued, before taking a puff from her pipe and falling away into another discussion, giving a final justification from a relativity that most outside of Ukraine will never understand.

I knew my explanation was probably impossible for her to rationalize, how the "other" side would perceive the photograph, or how any journalist outside of Ukraine would easily distort and twist the reality of this visual to fit their own narrative, a narrative from a world where the shoes of Ukrainian lives had never been worn nor walked in. I knew it wasn't my place to judge, and it certainly wasn't the right time for explanations. Because this wasn't my land being continually invaded. There was no room to care that a body had a mother who would never know what happened to her son. No room to consider that this soldier might not have wanted to fight in this war.

~

It's just meat. It's a phrase I heard not only to describe the dead of the enemy over the years, but to describe all who have died in Ukraine's war, whether comrades or enemies.

What's done has been done.

Is this what happens when life is continually a life of struggle, generations of genetically inherited trauma and war? Is that what Bizhan was now, just meat?

I don't understand why they lied to his family ...

I could still hear him saying it during his interview that day. And I could still see his face when he said it, how he was a few days unshaven. I could see his posture, hunched over in contemplation at the coffee table, and the way he first fell into a sort of grief or a loss for words, as if something finally broke his seemingly unbreakable animation.

"We can cry later," Misha wrote, responding to my guilt pushes, telling him that this can't be easy for you. Because it couldn't have been easy for him, or for any of them. For Misha, Babay, Vasya, Valkyrie, the Aidar crew who spent nights in my rental flats over the years, playing music and drinking into immature veteran oblivion, engaging in conversations until the sunrise, all differences in one another's countries, politics, ways of life, and perceptions colliding in these moments to create a space of absolute oneness.

I couldn't help imagining what Bizhan would have said to Misha in the moment, if it would change his mind, if Misha would then come forward and lay it out to Bizhan's mother as he had done for me.

He's dead.

Because Bizhan's mother was still searching for him, she still had hope, just as the mothers of the dead Russians scattered on the country road in Kharkiv probably had. And now I was caught in the middle of it when she started asking for my help. By hiding the details of a story that should have belonged to her, I was steering her sense of hope.

He's a smart boy, I know he's okay.

They posted photographs on Telegram. Photographs that they, the Russian soldiers, took of the remains of Ukrainian bodies after the ambush, the only evidence that may ever be received to identify the dead from that day. Because the Ukrainians couldn't go back and take the bodies, even though this was their land. It was occupied; no body exchanges, just the photos, enough for his comrades to confirm what they already knew, even though they couldn't see much more than a familiar shape wrapped in familiar clothing. But for his family, for his mother, for the public, officially, Bizhan was missing. And maybe Bizhan will always be missing. Maybe his mother will wait her entire life for him to bust through the door with his over-the-top laugh or walk into Valkyrie's flat and head straight to the bathroom for a foot washing to avoid her brutal hygiene scolding. I wonder if he'd find the humor in it all, being the mysterious man forever missing, and I can picture him writing a dark comedic chapter about it in the book he never finished, maybe deciding that it was the perfect ending.

I imagine the Russian soldiers going through his phone after they threw him into a ditch with the other bodies. Going through his phone logs, his messages, scrolling through the threads, scrolling past my most recent conversation with him, a rare English conversation, and maybe even laughing upon reading his words: "And you are increasing the chances for us to stay alive in the future," his response to my check-in: "still alive?" with an attached photo of the items he requested: Anemometers, thermal scopes, GPS rangefinders.

"Dead fucker, I'm angry at him," Babay said.

I understood this feeling of wanting him to come back for just one moment, wanting to shake him and punch him for dying, to tell him to stop playing war games, to get the hell out of this. But what choice did he have? What choice did any of them have? Except to eternally fight for justice in a world that was created for them and against them by leaders who have never been leaders, or leaders who've forgotten what it's like to be one of the people, leaders who've gotten lost along the way.

We're used to this. War will be forever, Misha explained.

Tell Jenn I changed my mind, I hate the Russians. I'll kill them all, Valera said to Valkyrie.

It might be another ten years, or maybe thirty years or fifty years, or maybe a lifetime before Lena looks at the photograph I took for her and questions the person she was in that moment. Just as I question the photos of myself posing in front of war ruins in Afghanistan. But it remains to be seen whether these men and women who fight for their land will ever be free of the cycle of those who send people to war.

A CRICKET IN POLAND

JUNE 2022
BRAMKI, POLAND

I killed a cricket in Poland. It was an accident, just an automatic slap to the neck to crush a nuisance crawling over my skin.

I saw its little green body fall to the ground by my feet, then told it I was sorry before carrying it to the nearby bushes, allowing the musical spikes of its still-intact leg to latch onto a leaf high off the ground. Just in case it was still alive, to keep it safe from another monster such as myself. And then I questioned my state of mind.

I wasn't the type to remove a spider from the corner of a room and set it free outside. I'd rather crush it into a smudge against the wall. Insects were soulless aliens, even if I preferred some species over others. In truth, the spider was often a target of intentional murder, sometimes by the hands of others at my arachnophobic pleas for help, but the insects of curiosity, the ones that I found small beauties within, they were simply whisked away after observation. The praying mantis, the fireflies I'd catch and put in a jar when I was a child, watching them light up like stars throughout the night on a bedroom shelf. Or the cricket, a creature of musical mystery when in its habitat, but a beast with power to whirl a human into insanity when lost inside the walls of mankind's structures. But none of them, not spiders nor fireflies nor crickets, had the power to invoke emotion from me in their death, whether intentional or accidental.

This damn cricket in Poland. The remorse was entirely out of place, but it wasn't unfamiliar. It took me back to a moment in my life, the second baby bird I found in one New Orleans spring. I saved him during an afternoon walk with my dog around the neighborhood, heard his little chirps of distress that lured me to the black cat who was closing in for a final act of torture.

That little bird. He even flew to me once, as if he recognized me as his safety. But then he died the next day, and I blamed myself for it. Maybe I didn't feed him right, maybe I didn't keep him warm enough, or maybe I put him under too much stress, the list goes on. I just knew that it had to have been my fault. There was no other way.

It wasn't long after my father died that this happened. But I didn't cry when my father died, at least not how I imagined I would have in the years before, when imagining a life without him. And when I think about his death, I don't feel the same visceral emotion that comes back to me every time I think of the little bird, a memory I try to avoid at all costs. But then this damn cricket made me feel it all over again.

It's interesting to again recognize that I have only one memory attached to this kind of visceral emotion when concerning the death of a human. It was during the summer of 2004.

Scott Corwin was new to the unit, the battalion's construction officer slotted for our next rotation into Iraq. He filled a void with Goldstein gone. I had a new smoking buddy on the back porch of the battalion headquarters, and although we didn't race down Highway 144, we sometimes took our Harleys out for weekend rides, and we never missed an opportunity to talk about girls in between our discussions about Iraq and wanting to get out of the Army.

He didn't want to go to Iraq, and he certainly didn't want to die in Iraq. He was full of life and had big plans for his future in the civilian world. But he ended up dying anyway, just not in the place where he feared death the most. He was murdered just a block away from his apartment on Forsyth Park, three blocks away from mine, right along a historic cobblestone path in one of Savannah's downtown squares. The police reopened the crime scene the very same morning, once the sun rose and just in time to cover it up from the tourist buses.

Dan Tranchemontagne died the next day, although I didn't officially know it until two months later, when I finally had the courage to call his house. I have plenty of photographs of him. We met during my first week in Kuwait, when we were getting ready for the big push into Iraq. He was always there with a cold Coca-Cola and an ear to listen when I returned on convoys to pick up supplies.

He seemed so old back then, in his 30s, and now I'm far older than my memory of him. A schoolteacher from Maine, he was a reservist who just had to finish a two-year rotation in the safest place to be over there, Kuwait, and then come home. Instead, he came home early, for Christmas, but not under "the best of circumstances," as he told me when he called from Walter Reed Army Medical Center. Not a gunshot wound, not an IED, just a spot on the skin neglected for too long. Melanoma put him in the ground only five months later.

When my little brother died a few years later, that was the first time I questioned myself. What the hell had happened to my emotions; he was only fucking nineteen years old, yet I didn't feel that same stab of death as I did for Scott and Dan. And I questioned myself again in Poland, how a fucking cricket evoked a feeling I had lost so many years ago for the death of a human, but not the death of Bizhan, of Iryna, of Demon, of the dozens of familiar faces that moved in living memories as if they were still alive, but now presented as frozen photographs attached to social media posts with the single lit candle.

The next day, I sat in the same chair outside, the chair I had been sitting in when I killed the cricket. Valkyrie was also outside, planting tomatoes and cucumbers; she always talked about having a garden in the countryside one day, just as her family had growing up in Pyatigorsk. I noticed something moving in the corner of my eye, down by my feet, and it was that cricket. It came back again, hobbling on its one intact leg. And again I questioned myself, how I could be so damn happy about it?

Yuliia Tolopa

Translated Excerpt from Interview
Toretsk, Ukraine, 2018 / Kyiv, Ukraine, 2019

YT: *This was probably the last thing that broke me at the time. My very good friend was killed, I can even say he was my brother. There was an explosion. A Grad missile landed and I was literally thrown out of my bed. The missile got into our bunk room, destroying half of it. I got up, the scenery was very ... as if from a film ... hot water gushing, pipes cracked, the nurse on the floor, screams. At that very moment, Chaika, shocked and covered in blood, ran up into the room saying that DJ's lying there.*

He always used to say: "Mom, don't worry, I have Yuliia, you know that if something happens to me, Valkiria will always bring me back." And so I brought him back home. To his funeral.

I was present at more than a hundred funerals of my combat brothers, but I will never forget this one. I found out that I was pregnant. I had strange thoughts about not willing to live ... I didn't know what to do ...

JT: *Why did you decide to have her?*

YT: *I was tired of death.*

115

How Do We Get Home?

May 2022
Kyiv, Ukraine

How to make it home? Where were the Russian tanks? Did they make it to the south of the city? Or did they close in on the western residential streets of Nivky, near my flat? It was a rare moment in life to feel subjected to the media's drone footage to gain a clearer landscape of my own neighborhood, my own home.

Piece by piece, contact by contact, tell me what you know, what you see around you, what you know to be true by standing there in the immediate proximity. Help us make the map to take us back where we belong.

A drive on the north highway might be faster, unless we get caught behind the farming trucks on the smaller, two-lane highway. Or a collapsed bridge might send us on a one- to two-hour detour on farm roads more suitable for off-roaders and tractors than cars. And an even longer detour if one of the cities ravished and pillaged—Irpin, Makariv, Borodyanka, or Bucha—is closed off for body removal, demining operations or removing unexploded artillery rounds from roads, sidewalks and playgrounds.

The E40, the southern and most well-paved highway in Ukraine before the invasion, has more lanes and less distance, but it's just as unpredictable. Burnt carcasses of tanks and vehicles litter the shoulders or sit in the center of a lane, unexpected shrapnel scars send cars swerving into accidents, new rocket attacks can turn a final hour of driving into four.

Is this still home? I wait in line for an additional two hours at the checkpoints in the city, at almost every major intersection. Left turn, checkpoint. Straight ahead, checkpoint, right turn, closed or blown-up gas station and then another checkpoint. Who are you today, a journalist? Or are you a volunteer?

Some days it's better to play the journalist card, especially near Kyiv or near the front line. Depending on the week, it can serve as a no-questions-asked pass when they're investigating war crimes and herding in journalists to prove Putin's evil. But farther west, near Lviv and Volyn, where the National Guard and newly drafted conscripts have nothing better to do than watch the war online and hope for a Russian soldier to pass through their post, it's a go-to-jail card most of the time. I'm a spy now; my footage must be confiscated. A scan of my passport shows I've traveled to Belarus within the year, a country I've never stepped a foot inside of, even when I tried over three years ago, on an ignorant road trip, knowing nothing of the country's political ties with Russia or the requirement for Americans to first obtain a transient visa.

"I can't do this anymore," Valkyrie said from the window ledge where she sat, smoking a cigarette, in the tiny kitchen of the small studio I rented. We'd been staying at the studio each time we came through Kyiv since early April, the first time we were able to return to the city. It wasn't far from our flat in Nivky, but we still opted not to stay there yet, even though the refugees from Bucha, whom we had allowed to live there after escaping the Russian occupation of their neighborhood, had left the previous day, taking their first step in gluing back the pieces of their lives. Taking the first step in a future that was about as predictable as the weather.

"I want to go home," she continued.

But she wasn't referring to the flat in Nivky, and I knew that Poland wasn't home in her heart. So then, where was home? In Poland, it was always Kyiv, but in Kyiv, this city of air sirens and checkpoints and sporadic bombings, it was apparent that we just didn't know anymore.

I wasn't ready to go yet, but I knew it was easier for me to stay longer, to continue driving east and work for a few days. Because nothing waited for me in Poland, now that my dog was gone. Only new supplies that hadn't yet arrived and a shoebox-sized apartment with too many children. Not only Valkyrie's daughter, but three more refugees we had taken in along the way: her daughter's classmate from school along with her one-year-old baby sister, and their mom. Six people in a tiny two-bedroom rental where the crying ricocheted off the walls and into my brain.

Staying was something entirely different for Valkyrie. We'd already finished our supply work earlier that day, shipping off boxes of donated medical kits, tourniquets, range finders, night vision thermals and the highly sought-after Motorola UHF radios through Ukraine's Nova Poshta to Kharkiv, Kryvyi Rih and other cities fighting on the front line. Valera had already come through in person to pick up his stash, in turn saving us with three canisters of diesel, enough for me to drive east to Kharkiv before we headed back to Poland. But then, where would that leave Valkyrie?

It was too much time for her. To sit and wait and remember. To be reminded of the guilt she still carried. That she wasn't there fighting with her comrades, that she had abandoned the country that finally gave her an identity, a passport and citizenship, only weeks earlier, right when they needed her most. It was too much time to internalize the social media hate comments, calling her out for not standing there with them on the front line, from soldiers fighting for Ukraine who didn't have children, who didn't know more than the heroic image of Valkyrie, the legendary Russian who fought for Ukraine. It was just too much time to be reminded that she couldn't stay forever, because she knew she had a responsibility back in Poland.

"If Max gets killed, I know she'll never stop, she'll want revenge," Valkyrie explained as we drove west toward the border.

Anya, Max's wife and Valkyrie's comrade from the earliest years in Ukraine, had sent one of the first messages to Valkyrie's phone as we waited in line to evacuate in February. She didn't have a car, but she had to get her child to safety.

After we left them in Kharkiv in April, I couldn't help wondering about their son, and how both mother and father were out there on the front line, sometimes sleeping under the same roof in a school-turned-base-camp that might get bombed, taking them both out at the same time.

"It's an addiction, Jenn," Valkyrie said, something she once described to me in a recorded interview years prior.

I will try to leave, but if my help is needed at the front, I will come back again. It's something you can't just abandon; it's like a drug. If you're on it, you can't go away from it. To quit you probably need a strong will, the understanding of why you're doing it, the realization that here within the peaceful life, there are people who wait for you. The most important thing is the people. The people who will help you escape.

We continued driving in silence, past the closed gas stations and burnt tanks and into the sunset west, the one stable beauty in a country at war.

BUTTERFLIES ON FIRE

APRIL 2018
KYIV, UKRAINE

A few months after we returned from Afghanistan in late 2002, while waiting for our orders to deploy to Iraq, I drove to Jacksonville, Florida, for an Ani DiFranco concert, drawn by a nostalgic memory of her on stage in Newburgh, New York, this symbol of power against the machine and everything I despised about West Point. Following her opening act, after the standing ovation and the whooping settled down, she embodied the same spirit of my nostalgia, going into protest over the president's controversial decision to invade Iraq. I was naive in forgetting that I was no longer the same person of my memory, a West Point cadet with big ideas about the world, ideas generated from a time when our country was at peace. I was naive in believing that protests over war would only protest against those who sent their soldiers to war.

"Patriots?" she scoffed. "Patriots aren't those who blindly follow."

My friend saw the words go through my gut like a bullet, throwing me back down into my chair as the rest of the crowd went into another standing ovation. Anger was my defense mechanism, swearing her off and ranting, my words wasted, muted by the overpowering cheer in the air. Because in another walk of life where I had never been sent to war, I probably would have been cheering her on with the others. And I wasn't proud. I didn't feel like a patriot, I didn't believe in the president's decision to invade, and I felt like a coward for hiding behind a military contract, for insisting that I didn't have a choice. Because making a choice meant going AWOL like our spineless chaplain had, months before we left. It meant breaking an oath, a promise, not to mention the possibility of going to military prison. It meant doing something extreme, taking a risk and sacrificing everything. Just as Ukraine's volunteers did in 2014.

Why did you go?

True and raw patriotism exposed through the axis question of my interviews with the 2014 volunteers.

In the beginning of the project, before sitting down at the table with a recorder, before spending countless hours of downtime with the volunteers, I imagined that their answers would reveal it all, this unquestionable purpose behind throwing themselves into the fire and the stark difference between our experiences in war.

"I often find myself asking the same question, why did I really go?" Alina told me a few months after our first interview.

She reminded me of my own inner dialogue and the years I spent analyzing and questioning my own memories and what role patriotism played in my wars. Not in why I went to Afghanistan, but within my memory of wanting to go and this brief feeling of pride I felt in serving our country. It's almost as if I wanted to prove it couldn't be true, partly because once we hit the ground, it became clear that the American public's perception of our presence there in no way matched reality. But it also wasn't synonymous with the person I knew myself to be, who rejected the applauds following Bush's vengeful war declaration, who innately distrusted politicians, who believed that war could never be the answer. And yet, I still remember wanting to go, believing there was a purpose to be found, something to make up for all the wrongs of 9/11.

"Butterflies on fire," Babay said.

"Butterflies on fire," Alina echoed. "Butterflies on fire, that's it."

"Butterflies sometimes fly into fire," Babay explained. "They think it's the sun. They're drawn to the heat, and they burn out. I compare this with war veterans. Some people are just drawn to the fire."

And I could feel the fire, standing there with them on the overlook of Independence Square, our group of veterans scattered among the other youthful gatherers, drinking whiskey colas and playing guitar, sitting on benches or on blankets thrown onto the grassy hillside. This was the place, the war before the war, the revolution. It happened right here, beneath us and in the aperture traveling past the Stella's cloaked, winglike arms, of Independence Monument, moving on across the fountains of the central square. Within their presence and their stories, it felt as if it were still happening, that it was brought back to life, its pulse vibrating through the night air in a parallel frequency. The same vibration that magnetized others to join and stand side by side with them in the revolution, including Ukrainians outside of Kyiv watching on television and people from around the world. They were a tribe brought together by the destruction of a world they had known before.

So much like 9/11, the only time we were attacked within our own borders. The only time my generation felt this kind of destruction and fear of what's coming next, the only time we turned inward and toward one another, across differences and demographics, instead of pushing away from one another. The only time I could identify with a feeling that some of the volunteers might perpetually live with every day, even when walking in the peace life, so long as the war continued, so long as the threat remained on their border.

"It's a sense of purpose," I chimed in. Because I knew the fire wasn't simply a death trap to burn us out. It was something larger than us, a purpose to match the new realities we lived in, in a world where the events we experienced were no longer something of the imagination.

There was a thread woven through us, an understanding that allowed me to stop fighting the memory of wanting to go to Afghanistan. Because I understood that motives for going to war, or wanting to go to war, aren't so black and white, and they aren't always defined by blanket themes of patriotism and country and protecting borders. Even in Ukraine, even for these volunteers who made the choice to go themselves in 2014.

I wanted to see what it was like ... .

Honestly? I just needed to escape my relationship.

The only reason I went was because my brother went. I had to be with him.

Because this is my land! My home!

How could I just sit aside? I had to do something.

Maybe the cloud of a never-ending war was the culprit of Alina's doubt, that their purpose on the Maidan and in the war was slowly washing away into a distance and without the resolution many had dreamed for, so much like my generation of 9/11 veterans gave way to one that moved on and away from it in a distant memory. But I could see something that perhaps many of them couldn't and wouldn't see for years to come. How could they not go to the front when the rest of their revolutionary tribe was there? And if I had been given the choice to decline my orders for Iraq, how would I have just abandoned my tribe, my comrades, and watch them go without me? And be left behind in the peace life, disconnected and in a disconnected world?

~

There's a point when you let go of the world you left behind. When you realize the hurt of expectations, that they'll only bring you pain, and you accept that your life at home must go on without you. Because if you don't let go, it's too easy to get angry—angry when they don't write often enough, or when after you wait in line for what seems like an eternity to reach that little makeshift wooden booth with the metal foldout chair and the black satellite phone, your only lifeline home, they're not there on the other end, waiting to hear your voice. When only hours earlier, you were on lockdown inside your tent, wondering if you'd be alive to see the light of day the next morning, or if instead you'd be skin and bone melted in with tarp rubber under the heat of a rocket-propelled grenade's combustion.

There's a point when you let go of the world you left behind, because you have to accept that your worlds are so far apart, that they can never be closer, and our experiences and understandings in life can only be relative to the world we're living in, and to the world we know and experience. So we become a new family until we can get back home to our own.

There's a point of letting go when you're over there, but I think we're tricked into believing that it's only temporary, and that what you're letting go of can come back to you one day.

IRYNA

They were buried right there. In the forest. A tall mound of dirt and two bodies, or what was left of them. Pieces of them. Placed in the earth by the man who found their remains scattered throughout the trees, the man who saw the Russian fighter jet release a missile that landed less than ten meters from where they sat in a vehicle together. Right there, in the outskirt forests of northern Kyiv, where so many gathered mushrooms in the spring and summer.

Listening to the silence there, the silence and the birds carrying on about their day, I imagined this was a place Iryna Tsvila, the woman of roses, of flowers and gardens, would prefer to rest. I could hear her voice, her voice and the ambient sounds of the birds I edited into her audio story, just like these birds in the forest, preceding her words that I chose to open with: "People, in order to plant roses on this land, we must first preserve this land."

We didn't remain in constant close contact after her interview, not like I did with many other volunteers over the years. There were brief encounters, always accompanied by tight embraces in lieu of a common language, and in between those moments, brief check-ins, asking for approval of her audio story or if she'd allow me to release her full interview to the Maidan Museum for its archives, because her story needed to remain in historic documentation.

Our brief communication over the years took nothing away from the impression she'd left on me during her interview and photo shoot. Understanding the full scale of her story through words in print would take months of transcribing and translation, and there was no way to convey everything in the moment as she spoke vigorously, full of passion, my unofficial interpreter, Alina Viatkina, struggling to keep up with her pace. But even without comprehension of semantics in the immediate moment, anyone would be able to sense the passion, complexity, strength, and beauty of her story by just sitting there and listening. Listening to this woman, nearing fifty, the only woman of her age I met, who was absolutely determined to fight in the revolution, to fight on the front line, to change the world she lived in, to free Ukraine into independence, to feel she had an eternal purpose in the world.

I didn't know she was with Demon, the soldier she was buried with, or that she had married him after I met her. He was much younger, but it made sense. Her age by number in no shape or form matched the spirit before my lens, a tornado of free-flying youthful energy, jumping and dancing and laughing after we finished the more serious and solemn photo session. After I said, "Ok, now just do whatever you want; these are for you."

I knew Demon, but only without Iryna. In fact, I had known him since the first day my feet walked up and down the steep slopes connecting Kyiv's city center streets to Maidan Square. He was always there with Babay, silent in the background, listening and laughing, raising his glass and chiming in for the toast, but his voice was never the dominant sound in conversations. It was as if he wanted to remain somewhat invisible, his presence only becoming apparent when leaving for the night, always bidding farewell with a handshake or a hug. They were the last-minute reminders, each time, that I also wanted to interview him one of these days. And that was always my parting question to him, up through the last time I saw him in the winter of 2021.

Why haven't I interviewed you? Let's please do this!

One of these days.

It didn't surprise me that Iryna would fight again. But never would I have imagined that she would be one of the first to fall after that day in February 2022. And never would I have imagined that it would happen not in that place that used to be considered the front line, in the Donbas, but in this place, a place we all used to call the peace life.

Even now, in this moment that we're standing here in the forest five months later, in front of the dirt mound where a memorial cross engraved with their names has recently been placed, this place isn't quite considered the peace life again. Even though the invading Russians have officially retreated from this part of the country, after absolutely demolishing its peaceful suburbs, and even though we all want it to be that place again, where we can try to move along again with a somewhat normal life, there's this looming sense of doubt and unknown in the air. It's an unspoken sadness as we stand there around the grave. In Babay's unwilling-ness to show emotion, in Alina and Vasya, who married days after the first missiles came through, distracting themselves with the puppy they rescued from the destroyed suburb of Borodyanka.

I watch Babay's mother kneel, watching a butterfly dance on the engraved names, allowing the first tears to fall in this moment. Not only in the grief of losing Babay's closest friend—Demon was practically her own—but in all the youth lost, in the sliced arteries and veins that once connected the 2014 community who survived over the years. In all those who might be gone next, in knowing that Babay was now conscripted to serve on the front line of the war. In this new sense of doubt brought by a war that has affected almost every living being across Ukraine, narrowing the divide be-tween the front line and the peace life, and in some places, entirely removing the divide. Because now, all of Ukraine was subject to becoming a front line. At any given moment. On any given day.

Are you safe?

The dominant question when standing outside the borders. And there isn't a real way to answer because there isn't a way for those outside the border to conceptualize the feeling when you're standing within.

There's no running. Those who have decided to stay have stayed, and for many, they simply cannot leave by law. And there's no hiding. We won't stop trying to live, to gather like old times, like we do now, sitting by the lake after visiting the grave, cooking shashlik and drinking toasts to memories. But now when we do this, we do it with a new understanding. That any one of us might be gone the next time we gather.

THE NAVIGATOR

JULY 2022
APOSTOLOVE, UKRAINE

I crouched down to take a better shot of a feral dog sleeping in the doorway of a newly transformed military base camp. Schturman crouched down, eye level and only inches from my face, too close to raise my camera a second time without whacking him with the lens. No interpreters or friends with limited English to help coordinate what was commonly an energy-packed conversation between us. It was just him and me this time, familiar territory and a moment he needed to unload everything that was eating away at him. Never had I hated the language barrier so much, or rather, hating myself for not becoming proficient in Russian by this point. It was a common badgering point between us.

Schturman, learn English!

Why can't you speak Russian yet! Learn Russian!

He won the debate without words, but Schturman, Russian for "Navigator," wasn't his usual semantic bundle of explosive energy this time around. He was calculated and paced, and even without comprehending each foreign word in the monologue he presented, I understood him. Through the familiar names he mentioned, through his body language, through his solemnness. Through the man I knew him to be from the previous four years.

"Are you saying you feel guilty because you left the Army and your soldiers? Or did I misunderstand you?"

"Da," he responded, not budging from the crouching position that was becoming quite uncomfortable on my knees.

He knew I'd understand. I was a constant presence from his former life in the 20th Battalion, but only former in the sense that he was physically removed, trying to inhabit this new atmosphere south of Kryvyi Rih, his native city. A city he barely frequented before the invasion and even now, no matter how close he was to his wife and home. He still managed to hide away in war, only now as one of the region's Territorial Defense commanders, defending the front line in southern Ukraine.

We'd talked about his struggle plenty of times over the years, the decision leading to this point, of whether or not to leave the Ukrainian Armed Forces. Each time I visited him on the front line, we always circled back around to this final topic of discussion over tea and cigarettes in the break tent. No doubt the topic was inspired by the question I presented to him the second time we met, when I recorded him on the positions of Avdiivka's industrial zone: "What will you do when the war ends? Do you imagine a place for you in the peace life?"

"I can't abandon the guys," he answered. "They are like kids. They can't function without me, and I cannot be without them either. For a time being, sure, no problem. And then I come right back."

He was known by all as the commander who would never leave the front, no matter the constant urging from his soldiers (who eventually gave up on it), to take a break, rest and reenergize. Only on a rare weekend would Schturman go home to visit his wife, barely breaking into his stash of accumulated leave days that would more than likely never be taken.

I can't. I'm the commander.

What if something happens when I'm gone?

Perhaps there was some truth in his rationalizing. I knew about his past and one of the stories that continued to haunt him. A rare ambush in 2014 that killed 20 of his comrades, an ambush coinciding with his rare absence, and not even his absence from the war, just from the immediate vicinity of his soldiers, when he was called to headquarters for commander duties.

But I also knew there was more to it than this. And he knew that I knew. How walking in the peace life was often like a performance, a funeral put on for the people by a family who might rather do without. To let the visitors line up and give condolences, to say their last words, to pray for them, nothing the survivors of the dead usually needed or wanted. And in the peace life, it was another act for the people of the peace life, for those who have never experienced the front line, going through the motions to fit in and appear normal, go to dinner with friends, play with the children, bring flowers to your spouse, laugh and smile, don't engage in political discussions about the war after drinking, and by all means, don't drink too much; it often turns to anger. But in our minds, we're somewhere else. Schturman's somewhere else. Back in the war zone, in his world with the comrades he'd been with since 2014, who followed him all those years, well into his volunteer battalion's integration into the Ukrainian Armed Forces. That was where living made sense... until it became too bureaucratic, too tangled in political agendas, egos and promotions. Too much like looking at the rear end of George Washington's statue at West Point. Perception is reality.

"There is nothing else we are capable of doing. I mean it. There's always somewhere to go to.... There's Iraq, there's Congo, Africa, there's, I mean..." he concluded in Avdiivka.

His solution was simple. If he left, they'd all leave together, and if there was ever an escalation, they'd come back together again. They'd fight together again. And if the war finally ended, there were other options, other wars to fight somewhere in the world. Somewhere they could continue to carry that same sense of purpose and carry it together.

There was no way Schturman could have predicted the impossible becoming possible, that Russia would launch a full-scale invasion only a few months after his contract finished. No way for him to discern that this escalation was a true threat after eight years of escalation normalization.

It was the first time I was without a response for him. No uplifting message to counter his guilt or the reality that his soldiers who were still in the 20th Battalion were struggling, dying, falling apart without the glue of their leader. And for the first time, I felt absolutely hopeless, that there was nothing more I could do to help or change the situation, only deliver supplies and take photographs in a country that would clearly be stuck forever in a cycle of war. In understanding that this was their reality, to be well-trained victims of Russia terrorizing them for centuries, and that most of them would never have a chance to find a purpose outside of war.

"How do you do it?" Schturman had once asked me, referring to how I was able to move on in the peace life. If he'd asked me the question three years earlier, I wouldn't have been able to answer so simply: "I came to Ukraine."

THE TERMINAL

REFLECTION ON FEBRUARY 2002
KANDAHAR, AFGHANISTAN

When I try to remember Afghanistan, it's like an old reel of film, where most of the frames are blurred. As it turns, I can only get a general idea of what's going on, the background story, the people in motion. But then in between the blur, a frame comes into focus, showing the details, the emotions, before it transitions back into the blur. There are specific moments that I remember so clearly, and there are some that sit right on the edge. When I dig into the past further, when I talk to someone who was there with me, or maybe even when I look at a picture, the frames that were on the edge of focus become clear, and then the blurred frames become clear, one at a time. But what complicates this all, is that even when the frames come into focus, letting me see the emotion, I lose their place in time. When I feel the fear, or when I feel the tension; is it what I felt then, or is it what I feel now, remembering? Or is it both?

~

I know I was scared in Kandahar. I remember it very well, even though I often can't find the emotion. The memories attached are still very present, and they are often the most clear, the in-focus frames on an old reel of film that bring back the sights, smells, and sounds. Like the explosions. There were always explosions in Kandahar, sounding off day and night, echoing through the desert and shaking the ground and our tents when we tried to sleep. But it's the first blast, the memory of hearing it that allows me to tell the story, to paint the surrounding details. Now I can feel the stillness of the air, see the rare blueness of the sky that day, hear the saw blades running and the pieces of wood falling to the ground. I can taste the dust, smell the freshly cut wood; I can see the lines in Sergeant McKinney's weathered face and the blue-gray of his eyes

131

when I asked him, "What was that?"

It was so quiet that day. If anyone were to come in and check on us, we'd know well in advance by the sound of heels clicking against the tile floor, echoing through the empty hallways and funneling into our location.

We called this place the terminal, but the blue letters on the sign outside, hanging from those oddly futuristic, sand-colored, caterpillar arches called it the Kandahar International Airport. I'm sure it was a busy place once upon a time, but now we were the only ones there.

It was myself, Staff Sergeant McKinney, Sergeant Neal, and a few other soldiers from my platoon who had also arrived on one of the first few chalks, working in an open courtyard area that connected the main terminal to its surrounding corridors and buildings of the airport. My soldiers set up a hasty workbench there with their circular saw and tools, gravitating toward the only area offering the warmth of sunlight, and we'd spend the day chasing the moving beams, squeezing into the smallest places to soak in the last seconds of heat before the shadows of a desert winter returned.

I was sitting on the edge of a dried-up fountain, smoking cigarettes and listening to their casual side chatter as they sawed away at sheets of plywood; it was the kind of babbling you hear with a group of old friends playing cards, except this smack talk revolved around the arrival of our higher leadership on ground, the big brass and stripes that back home were often removed in a faraway office in a headquarters building, disconnected from the everyday ins and outs of a platoon or a company. Now in close proximity, in a tent city right down the dirt road, they were too much rank without enough to do, proving authority and destroying functioning systems while often displaying nothing remotely close to the kind of leadership I expected in a war zone.

I'm sure the conversation was instigated by the reason that we were up there in the first place, to build "VIP rooms" in the main terminal of the airport. VIP rooms. It felt wrong even thinking those words, let alone speaking them out loud. That this was the priority, our big service to the country, to build luxuries for "VIPs" in what was obviously slated to become the most luxurious living area within the perimeter. And who were these unnamed VIPs, anyway? The highest-ranking officers deployed to Kandahar? The visiting politicians who would swoop down to get a two-minute segment on national television, showing their faces in harm's way with the soldiers before hightailing it on the first flight out?

"Why don't you come with us, Ma'am," Sergeant McKinney said more than asked, trying to smooth out a frustration that he'd already mentally overcome, that there was nothing we could do to change the situation. Hours later, we were walking through the ghostly vacant hallways of the terminal like sole survivors of some post-apocalyptic world, following a trail of natural light that led us into the courtyard.

I never would have imagined that the terminal would become a place I could associate with tranquility. During our days on lockdown at Fort Stewart, even before we received our deployment orders, the blue letters and sandy arches were a constant backdrop on the national news, a daily visual that flashed by again and again, right alongside footage of the towers crumbling and the people falling through the sky. It became a symbol of the time, of the fear of war and the violent world where we were being sent; a hotbed of hate where we were wanted dead.

Maybe it was the unchallenged emptiness of it, or the details familiar of a civilized world, like the modern, tile floors, or the swimming-pool-shaped fountain. Or maybe it was the seemingly protective wall created by the arches of the buildings surrounding us in the courtyard, or the planted trees that offered a new dimension of color to the landscape. Whatever the reason may have been, it allowed the terminal to transform into something else when we were there, even if only for a moment. No longer was it the source of anxiety, but an escape from it, a quarantine from the rapidly intensifying energy of tent city where a blend of unspoken fears and uncertainties were all packed into a too-small, unvented space. It was our own quiet place, and the only place in Afghanistan where I can actually remember hearing the sound of birds chirping. I can still hear them now, in between the high-pitched sounds of the circular saw finishing its cut through a piece of wood. They are the last sounds I hear before the silence that introduces the first explosion.

BIZHAN SHAROPOV

EXCERPT FROM INTERVIEW
KYIV, UKRAINE, 2018

When the Russians entered with the regular troops, the war
totally changed. The artillery shelling became like it was in the
Second World War. I've never seen such a great picture, two
batteries of Grads [missiles] firing at each other. It looks like
a hurricane, you know, cause, it's something that cannot be
translated through a movie. When the shell explodes ... it beats
on your ears, it beats on your bones.

Cannot Be Translated

September 2022
Bakhmut, Ukraine

A photo cannot capture it. Perhaps video at least gives the dimension of sound. But no multimedia tool, not photo, video, or audio, can measure the feeling of the devastation. The smell of death that saturates the forest, even through the mask that I wear. The dog searching for his master, sniffing the ground and the scattered sheets of plastic and cloth that remain in the graves, sniffing the earth where a body was exhumed or remained to be exhumed—because I can see that the exhuming is nowhere near finished, no matter what the official statements claim. Just twenty-five meters away, in an abandoned Russian fighting position, there's a mound of earth marked with a cross made of tree branches.

A Soviet S-300 surface-to-air missile has a high-pitched blast when targeting the earth, a clapping like two garbage can lids smashing together. At least that was what it sounded like when the explosion woke me out of a dead sleep, even through the tactical earplugs I wore to successfully zero out the snoring of Ira's driver, who slept on a cot just a few feet away from me.

Ira warned me that this was one of the hottest areas of the fighting, that it was extremely dangerous, that she'd never seen anything like it in all her years as a war press officer, before the 2022 invasion or since. The day I arrived, she'd just returned from a tour of the city with journalists who certainly got the action they came for, running for cover in a building as the shelling began to fall around them. She showed me the photos of what remained of their car, what would have remained of them if they had been inside.

"I asked them not to publish this, because I'm worried the press center will close the area to journalists if they see it," she said.

"I think they're trying to kill me," she concluded, clearly shaken, not only by the close calls for her life or the smell of the exhumed corpses from the mass graves still lingering in her nostrils, but by the death of her childhood friend, killed in action the previous day. And still I found myself toting along behind her on a photo opportunity that wasn't even my own, but her job for the morning, to shoot portraits of tankers on the front line of Bakhmut. For Ukrainian Armed Forces billboards.

"Can you please drive now?" she said as we approached the checkpoint into the northern area of the positions, a request I wished she'd made after the second of three stalls in the middle of the road on the way. It became clear why she felt helpless without her driver and why she was already softening on her stance on allowing his return, even after the conflict from the previous night that ended with her calling the MPs. A bout of divorce and war depression, too much alcohol followed by threats to pull the pin from the grenade in his hand before running out the door with his loaded AK to continue the binge.

The shelling began before we reached the final checkpoint, and as we slowed down to give the daily passcode, the soldier waved and signaled us to continue without stopping, keep moving and get the hell out of there.

"Pull over," she said.

"Where?"

"We should go ... "

"Okay!"

"No wait, look ... "

"Ira, where do you want me to go?" I demanded as the shelling continued. It wasn't a good time for conflicting messages or misunderstandings, to say the least.

"Back up, you must see this, through the tree line."

I looked.

"Now we should keep going."

If I had stopped longer, if I had parked and taken the photograph, one would only see the streaks of smoke snaking across and down through the sky like jellyfish tentacles. And if I'd recorded video, they'd also hear the pounding and sizzling whooshes of metal launching into the air and the silence preceding a succession of blows as they imploded across the earth in fire. But without being there, without feeling the moment, the vibrations, the thuds, the intensity, it was all just sound and smoke in the sky. It was just a repetition of what's been seen and heard so many times before, in this war and every war around the globe.

When I walk through the destruction in Ukraine, I'm often taken back to my deployments with FEMA, shooting disaster and destruction. Each shot always concluded with a sinking feeling as I put down my camera, because there was just no way to measure the vastness of it all. I felt as if I were robbing its justice by presenting my images to the public, and in turn downgrading the stories of those who survived through it, no matter how hard and in how many ways I tried to frame the shot. And as the weeks passed, I found myself becoming numbed by it all, desensitized by the same image again and again and again. Just as the world outside was again becoming desensitized to Ukraine. Just as I was becoming desensitized, unless I happened to walk through the reality in the moment of occurrence, rather than after. Because after the moment, it was often just another hole in the ground. Another dead body. Another targeted school or a residential building with its guts and a family's last scene of dinner or breakfast hanging out and into the wind, where the missile had dissected the building clear in half, like a cross-section view of a medical dummy. And the school that was decimated only one kilometer away from me in Druzhkivka, it also looked like every other photograph of destruction. Except for me, this photograph was attached to a feeling, the experience of its detonation.

The external viewers of conflict easily become desensitized. Those who stand within it often become habituated. And those who push the buttons, who pull the triggers, are not only habituated and desensitized, but disconnected.

"Have you ever seen the face of someone you killed?" I had asked Valkyrie when I met her at the Route 66 gas station outside of Toretsk, just a few days after I interviewed her in 2018. It was the only response I could come up with after she boasted before and after footage of her work as a drone operator on her phone: video aerials of the target, and then aerials of the target as a missile came down from the sky upon it, turning it into a cloud of black smoke.

I thought about that day for years, what she thought about my question in the moment, if she imagined a face or felt a shred of humanity, or if there was simply not enough time and separation from the conflict. Because I knew how easy it was to normalize it all in the moment of war, whether defending your own land or being an invader on another's land. To kill the faceless enemy or to be killed by the faceless enemy. We're all in the mentality of self-preservation.

It reminded me of Kandahar, constantly on lockdown in our tents in full battle rattle, waiting for the explosions and the air horn and the predicted RPGs to fall. Explosions in the distance somewhere, earthshaking aftershock, cots and metal canteen cups and government-issued plastic rattling within the tarp walls of the tent. Immediate stillness and silence always followed as we waited for an explanation.

It's just a flare. Go back to sleep.

The flare was the easiest to become something beautiful, like fireworks in the sky. I remember being outside of my tent one night during the moment of detonation, and I caught the brilliance of the opening flash before the speed of sound. I can still see the picture in my mind, this white light illuminating a section of faraway landscape, morphing it into a macro photograph or a painting under a microscope, exposing details by the harsh contrast of white light and shadows; details that never came forward during the day. I saw little black dots, scattered throughout the canvassed section of the mountain, and even though I think they must have been trees, or the shadows of trees, I swear I saw a few of them moving before the curtain of blackness fell and the flare faded; as if they were little figurine soldiers, moving in a giant sandbox.

There were many nights and days on lockdown in our tents, hiding together under a tension-filled tarp, just listening and waiting for it all to end. No hitting the latrine, no visiting other tents, don't get caught if you're out for a smoke break. Only the air horn was an exception to leave, and no one wanted to hear the air horn, because that meant run for the trenches. Run for the trenches and hunker down low, hunker down low and pray that a defensive crouch, curled up in a ditch with your hands over your head will be all you need to survive the blast of a rocket propelled grenade. Pray that zero of the predicted three hundred rockets for that night will land anywhere within a ten-meter range of you, that they'll land far enough away to only feel the earth shake and the distant heat of fire; far enough away for shrapnel to only ricochet off your helmet instead of lodging into your exposed flesh.

"Yeah, this is comfortable, we'll sleep great tonight, no problem," I joked to Lieutenant Wilson, trying to lighten things up one night. We were side-by-side on our cots in our ten-man tent, lying on our backs in full battle rattle, staring at the ceiling, our heads locked into a cricked position by the chin straps of our helmets that weren't meant to stay on while in the position of sleep. It was the only thing to do while we waited, instead of thinking about death, about home, or for Wilson, about the newborn child she left back home only weeks before. Better to laugh at the absurdity of it all, of not only trying to fall asleep in our boots, helmets, flak vests and full gear, but at the notion that we'd be able to sleep at all during a potential rocket shower that could melt us into the landscape.

There were other times in Kandahar when we knew we were being attacked somewhere along the perimeter, and all I could do was pray that our weapons would remain an unused last resort, that we'd stay engineers for another day and let the infantry handle the fighting. But on any given night, if you went outside and listened over the loud whirling of the generators, you could hear the popping of gunfire and explosions and let it sound as far away as the toy soldiers in the sandbox, under the light of the flare.

Artillery warfare made it far too easy. Drone warfare made it even easier. To entirely remove ourselves from the havoc created by war. In the same way that those who send us to war are removed from the dead bodies that come home to broken families in coffins.

It's not their son or daughter. It's just a willing patriot. It's just a soldier. It's just meat.

But even in the proximity of an enemy, when we're close enough to see a face, war still has a way to remove it. I never thought I would be faced with the fear of confrontation or the decision to pull the trigger at close range. But so it happened, there was one night toward the end in Afghanistan when most of the company was gone. The few of us left sensed a breach of our immediate perimeter, a threat rustling in the darkness, moving closer. I remember lying there in the prone, heart pounding, finger on the trigger, ready to shoot an enemy with a face. There was no fear in this moment, no thinking or room for humanity, no hesitation. Only self-preservation, reaction, motion, moving, adrenaline. Defending. To kill or to be killed. By a human whose face we've removed because we're wired to believe he's the enemy, instead of the enemy being the one who sent him to kill us.

Voices

I'm a photographer. But really, I'm just a human drawn toward the truth, in snapshots of truth. Sometimes through sight, sometimes through writing, sometimes through capturing ambient sound and sometimes through recording voices. Voices that speak the truth of a life lived, that can remove differences and borders and racial divides rather than creating them. Voices that need to be preserved as a truth of history for years to come. Voices that can tell us the stories we regret we never asked. Voices that make you feel as if you're still standing with a person, long after they are gone.

Before we left for Afghanistan, I bought a small voice recorder and packed it in my footlocker along with packages of Ramen, cartons of cigarettes, disposable cameras and extra rolls of 35mm film. It was the kind you could buy from the small electronics section of a Walgreens or a CVS, an old school, portable Sony with microcassette tapes and sound quality that later proved horrible for anything past a voice note.

I can't remember why I felt a need to bring one with me, outside of having this perpetual drive to preserve and document everything in my life, and sound was a sense I always felt most connected to, it offered a different dimension of memory and nostalgia that looking at a photograph did not. I didn't use it often when I was there, but when I did, I recorded the ambient sounds surrounding us, the gunfire and explosions, the leadership briefings, the smack talk and banter between my comrades or even between myself and my soldiers. And sometimes when alone in the tent, I recorded my own voice, quietly talking to someone on the other side, in the other world, a written letter in voice without rehearsal, a letter that I never sent home. I imagine I was trying to preserve my own voice

142

as a memory for them, just in case I didn't make it home.

"I never met him but for some reason felt as if I did in some way. It's hard to explain," the volunteer transcriber of Bizhan's recording wrote to me. Beguiled by his voice and story, she followed him on Facebook over the years and must have noticed the months on end of silence, the primary posts on his account coming from his mother during her search for his whereabouts.

Her comment reminded me of the earliest years of my project when strangers from the Ukrainian community around the world volunteered to transcribe and translate the hours on end of audio recordings. I imagine the voices of the volunteers became sealed in their memories, just as they had in my own, intensified by the process of replaying the clips again and again to annotate every single word; the devotion of time required for transcription is often miscalculated by a newcomer.

The exhibit in Kyiv was to be the first time we'd play the voices of the volunteers to the public. But now, instead of listening to them in a museum or an institute while looking at their portraits, I'm sending them to family members and comrades of those who have passed on. Even the in-between moments, the photographic snapshots and snapshots in audio form, Bizhan and Babay and even Valkyrie playing guitar and singing, the celebration and banter between all of us together, the subtle nuances and details of a voice that makes each human unique. The purpose they are serving was unintended, and, to be brutally honest, beyond painful at times. Because never did I imagine a day when I'd stand in a Kyiv cemetery and watch the procession line at Bizhan's funeral, throwing handfuls of dirt in a grave beneath the portrait I made of him cradling his guitar. But it's the kind of purpose my work can serve in the moment without misinterpretation, and it's quite possibly much larger than I ever imagined, in the way I might have imagined the purpose of recording my voice in Afghanistan, played in the times when we are overtaken in fear that we've forgotten the sound of a lost loved one's voice.

But even before the invasion abandoned the opening, it had already become clear that the message I wanted to share might never break through the sound barrier in a country where the war was such a life force. It's irrelevant, at least now, because the one purpose I thought it might serve is no longer relevant. The divide between the front line and the peace life has been compressed through a struggle of war that's now been experienced by Ukrainians across the boundaries of what was once considered the peaceful life. And the divide between the veteran and soldier community? They were once again brought together by their shared fight, even though it might fall apart in time, once the moment of coming together runs farther and farther from our memories, once the war smooths out and converges into not a "full-scale invasion," but into the same, never-ending war that began almost ten years ago, tangled in politics and bureaucracy, only now with a twisted and elevated sense of what's normal or should be expected in a twenty-first-century war.

Regardless of the exhibit or publication opportunities, I'm content in realizing my work, my contributions, don't really have a finish line. It's not something for the immediate moment, but something that becomes appreciated by the smallest few in different moments, like those snapshots and handwritten letters in ziplock bags. And maybe it will be appreciated by the larger few years and years later, a testament of truth in war that connects all those who experience war.

Dog, Child, Owl

I cannot understand it, at least the entirety of it. Of why I left Ozliiv and crossed the border into Poland that first time. Because I truly wanted to? Because of an inability to withstand my mom's crying and panic? Because I felt I had no choice?

I didn't want to accept that the days of running solo were over. Ukraine was my land of freedom, of running rogue without carrying the responsibilities that weighed me down back in the US. It was the place where working wasn't work, where I had zero distractions, only passions to chase and spirits to be awakened, again and again and again. It was the freedom I hadn't realized I sought when I had been counting down the days. The freedom I erroneously believed would embrace me by the simple gesture of leaving the Army and joining the peace life. But then I brought my dog into my freedom. He was my only stability through all my impulsive moves and sporadic journeys over the previous fourteen years. He had been there when I finished wearing the uniform, through my love affairs and breakups and fuckups, through heartbreaks, thrills, family mental crises and death. I knew I couldn't continue like I had been, leaving him in New Orleans for months on end while I chased my love affair with Ukraine, especially during the last months or years of his life. So there was no other choice; he had to come to Ukraine with me.

I drove for hours these last few weeks. First from Warsaw to Kyiv, only a rare nine- to ten-hour straight shot, an amazing feat to actually avoid the unpredictable and highly probable five- to fifteen-hour add-on at the border, and not because of a massive exodus of refugees as in late February. Now it was simply an incompetence and attitude problem of government employment, overextended tea breaks, end-of-the-month quotas to fill and a few disconnected assholes who gloated over holding power over one's ability to cross the invisible line separating a country at war from a country at peace. Because they knew there was nothing anyone could do about it.

I rested a few days in Kyiv before driving the next ten hours to Bakhmut in the Donbas, to photograph Ira's brigade fighting on the front line and drop off some supplies, and five days later back to Kyiv. Only the return to Warsaw through the unpredictable border remained.

Google Maps had already failed me plenty of times since the invasion. It couldn't keep up with the shifting wartime changes, what bridge or road had been bombed or repaired, what posts had been abandoned or transformed into roadblocks of old barricades, burnt vehicles, concrete bastions, stacked tires, and mountains of sand.

Against the grain, I decided to take the E40 instead of the two-lane north road, despite knowing it was generally a stable route, despite Google's endless and dismissed reminders of a "faster route now available." But then I gave in somewhere near Rivne, just feeling chancy, a flip of the coin, craving the apparition of time moving faster with new scenery. Slowing down along the curved exit and dropping onto a narrow, two-lane countryside highway that descended and ascended straight into kilometers worth of a depth of field, I immediately regretted my decision. No matter the kaleidoscope of autumn colors, the swarming black clouds of swallows breaking through pockets of vivid oranges and reds and yellows and greens of leaves and earth saturated in color by the perfect geometry of sun and clouds and a cotton-candy-blue sky. It only deepened the knife in my gut and dropped me further into a time portal, dumping me right back on that fucking road almost nine months earlier, the same road that took me to Ozliiv, getting lost in the winter blackness, the pressure of my dog's anxiety building in the back seat as the drugs wore off and he came to awareness.

They say dogs need routine, they breathe routine, and for older dogs, it's what keeps them healthy and happy in the last years of their lives. I absolutely failed him in that regard. Upping him from Kyiv, I can still see him there, the look of utter confusion mixed with "not again, but don't leave me, either way," as I took the last bags to load into the car from a ghostly apartment empty of a loud six-year-old child and the scent of fresh-baked chicken coming from the kitchen where he'd stood at Valkyrie's feet, waiting for handouts that a dog at this stage in life is entitled to, in bulk.

Ukraine was supposed to be his last home, a final place to give him back that same stability he gave to me. But even before the invasion, before taking him from Kyiv, I moved into three different apartments in only two years. And the last apartment was sure to be the last. I had promised to keep him there until he died. Fuck, we moved there specifically for him. A rare ground-level flat in a green area; no more carrying him up and down flights of stairs, past the flat babushkas who adored him and patted his head every time we came through, identifying with this love for an elder that every elder deserves.

Each kilometer driving was a reevaluation of all my decisions. Was I selfish to move him to Ukraine? Maybe he would have been better, would have lived longer if I had just stayed at home in New Orleans, if I had stopped leaving him all the time. Better health-care, his dog friends, routine, and what he wanted most, me. He didn't have that much time left; couldn't I have sacrificed just a year or so?

After he died, I spent hours on end going through years of my phone backups on Dropbox, going through over a decade of phone snapshots and saving them to my computer. He dominated every month and year on the timeline—my number one model. I never stopped photographing him. But then in 2018, I noticed there weren't so many of him anymore. They were replaced by photographs of Ukraine. And when I looked at the dates in between the sparse clusters of him, in between photographs of Ukraine, I realized just how much I left him that first year.

It seemed as if it were all leading up to this. The feral dog I photographed at the mass graves in Izium, sniffing the holes in the ground where bodies had been exhumed, sniffing the piles of earth for a familiar scent, the scent of routine, the scent of his master. Or the dead dog in the middle of the road when I left Bakhmut, a black and white collie with a collar around his neck, left to the birds tearing away at his flesh. I stopped on the shoulder a half kilometer later. I couldn't get him out of my head, that what if, just what if he was still alive? What if I could still help him? I drove back, but there was nothing to be done.

I didn't drive all the way into Poland from Kyiv. After reaching the border control line that extended well past its usual point, after not moving an inch for two hours, I knew staying would be an overnight affair, one that I didn't have the physical or emotional energy for without a break from the gravel.

It didn't ease up the next morning. As a matter of fact, I could have sworn that I pulled up and parked behind the same car as the previous day, and in the exact same location on the road, under the same glaring, overcast sky that bore into my temples and behind my eyes.

My hopes were that by jumping into the line before noon, I'd make it across the border before the 18:00 October sundown, saving enough sunlight to escort me through the ninety minutes of unlit farm roads extending past Poland's border towns. But the window was well closed more than ten hours later, when I finally exited the last gate into the blackness.

For more than an hour I successfully dodged wild dogs, cats, and foxes darting in front of my headlights to cross the road. Only fifteen minutes remained to reach the main highway and the lights of civilization. Fifteen minutes and then I'd hit the fast road, pick up speed and make it to the hotel in Lublin before the kitchen closed. But then an owl dropped out of the sky less than one meter in front of the car, gliding peacefully before thudding into my windshield.

I searched in the darkness for his body, using my cell phone flashlight in the places my headlights couldn't reach, in the ditches shouldering both sides of the road and even in the overhanging tree branches. But only his feathers remained, scattered across the concrete and blowing into the air with the tailwind of a trucker who pulled over past me, making sure I was alright.

The chance of hitting a bird while driving is one in five thousand. What was the universe trying to tell me? In all this guilt I already carried, in all the good I was trying to do at every turn to save an animal, I killed an owl. Blinded him with my headlights, took away his defense mechanism to fly in the other direction.

"Maybe he's still alive," Valkyrie said when I called her in dismay. "It's not your fault."

But it was my fault. Maybe I should have driven slower. Maybe I would have found him if I searched longer. Maybe if I had a real flashlight in the car among all of the other tactical gear. I had my chemical mask and helmet and class IV body armor and first aid kit, but no decent flashlight?

Before we left Kyiv in February, I had found my dog hiding in the bathroom. Twice. Facing away from the door, so nothing could hurt him, so it wasn't possible to come inside, or so he imagined. The only time I had ever seen him do this was in New Orleans a few years earlier, when I came to pick him up from the house where my ex and I had lived, the house where I was no longer welcome to live. My ex was gone, but the house was destroyed, destroyed in anger over me, over my love affair with and in Ukraine. It looked as if an F-5 tornado had torn through it, except tornadoes don't punch holes in walls with clenched fists and hammers. I walked through and around the broken glass and destruction in the entry room, straight through the kitchen and down the shotgun hallway to the bedroom at the end, calling for him. In a panic I finally looked in the bathroom and found him facing the wall in the corner, waiting for the storm to end.

In Ukraine, it was because of Valkyrie's anger. Even in the last years of his life, when the dimension of sound was no longer a problem for his deaf ears, when thunder and fireworks no longer sent him into a shaking frenzy, he still felt her anger, heard her anger. Don't get me wrong. He loved her, he absolutely loved her, but in her anger he was frightened. I was frightened. And when I think of it again, I feel guilt, regret. Did I do the right thing, putting him with me in the turbulence of Ukraine? Did I really think the freedom I felt in this country would never be doused with swaths of darkness?

In the weeks before he died, it was Valkyrie who told me, *maybe you need to stop this time. Stay home with Cuba. Don't keep going back to Ukraine. Not now.* It was Valkyrie who said, *maybe you can go alone this time and I'll stay with him. If something happens while you're gone, you'll never forgive yourself.*

She was right.

Even in Poland, I still didn't give him stability. Forty hours in line to cross the border, then another four hours to the Airbnb in Warsaw where emergency veterinarians would rush to the flat twice, saving him from fluid in the lungs. Fluid in the lungs from his heart working too hard, from the stress of everything. Both times they came, they didn't think he'd make it to the next day. They told me to be prepared for his death. They were amazed when I brought him into the office the next week for the follow-up they never thought he'd live to attend.

I tried extending the time on the flat without success, not because it was a great place for him, but to prevent moving him again, stressing him again. But then move we did, only two weeks later, way out in the countryside of Warsaw.

It was a nice place for him, ground level and on a lake, and Cuba loved the water. He grew up on the water, on the Wilmington River in Savannah. But he couldn't walk all the way to the water, even though it was practically right out the door, a handful of meters away. So I'd carry him there, and I wish I'd done it again on the day we put him to sleep. I wish I'd done it every day, and that I'd stayed home with him every day during those last weeks, that I had sacrificed my need to go back into Ukraine.

I wasn't ready to give up my freedom. And I wasn't ready to leave Ukraine. But leaving Ukraine, separating myself just a little, allowed me to see more. That maybe Valkyrie's anger wasn't only her own. Maybe I had a part in it, in drinking too much when I told her not to, in letting the stress of the situation eat away from under my skin and break free into the air. Because often the stress revolved around Valkyrie, her mental health or anger, or how I wanted her to fix her issues and get better. But most often it revolved around Valkyrie's daughter. The daughter I had encouraged her to be a mother for when she finally made the decision to leave the Army. The daughter I had encouraged her to take responsibility for, and in turn give up the freedom we both found in war.

Veterans Day

THERE WAS A TIME IN MY LIFE when you could have asked me what month of the year Veterans Day falls within, and I wouldn't have had a clue. Even when I was in the Army, Veterans Day was just a four-day weekend, a break from waking up at the crack of dawn for four consecutive mornings. It wasn't until years later, well after finishing my service, that I began to pay more attention, as if it suddenly dawned on me that not only was I a veteran, but I was a combat veteran, and there was actually a day in the year to honor my kind. And then suddenly, every year on November 11, I began tuning into social media, watching it flood with posts from fellow soldiers as we thanked one another for our service, telling one another we're proud to have served together in combat, wishing one another a happy Veterans Day, posting old photographs from that time in our lives. I found a sanctuary there, but at the same time this new realization metastasized into an internal dilemma of rationalizing my expectations, because I suddenly had expectations. Expectations of my family and friends, of those in the civilian world who knew I had worn the uniform, to acknowledge Veterans Day, to remember it, to say "thank you for your service" on November 11 ... because they never did. Despite the firehose of radio and media announcements, parades, Veterans Day discount ads in store windows, spam emails, magazines, newspapers and television ads, no one connected the dots. And I resented myself for letting the expectations consume me, to let it bother me that I had to remind them every year, to remind my brother that "Memorial Day is not the day to tell me thank you for your service, you idiot. It's a day to honor the fallen!" Because I knew good and well that had I never served a day in a combat zone, I would be no different from them. And I also knew that they didn't really know what they were thanking me for, other than a perception of heroism or patriotism. So how was it justified for me to be angry or hurt simply because I had become a part of a world that they would never understand?

It's a bizarre moment, standing in a COVID-safe corner of an elevator at the VA medical center in New Orleans, casually chatting with a Korean War vet and a Vietnam vet, three generations of wars from different walks of life, and realizing that I could identify with something that had once been so foreign to me, like the old men I used to see as a child at the Fourth of July or Memorial Day parades, wearing their veteran hats and insignia pins and buttons and patches, driving their cars with the "Vietnam Veteran" bumper stickers. And even more interesting to realize that I often felt more connected there, in the elevators and in the waiting rooms at a stupid hospital, than I did in the world outside, where my community had spread out all over the world. Because there, inside the waiting rooms, inside that elevator, no walls divided us, only a universal block of space and time that separated each one of us from our wars. We were no different from one another, beyond the obvious factors of age, skin color, culture and bringing-up, the things that are most often obscured or omitted when together in a war zone. Things that remain obscure when we leave our wars and meet each other again in the peace life.

Moving in and out of Ukraine allowed me to see more clearly. That in the end, it's not our individual countries or patriotism that defines us but an experience. That we become something larger, a universal tribe with a universal memory of war that shapes the way we move through the world forever. The same struggles, the same fears, the same regrets, the same brotherhood molded under a system of survival, a system that creates a choosing of sides. And once we reach this point along the timeline, we have an awareness that allows us to let go of pride, of anger and regret, of the isolation many of us find ourselves trapped in as we move forward in the peace life. Because we realize, there really is no such thing as transitioning, at least not in the way we imagined before. There's no process with an end state, no sudden and seamless reunification with the world we left behind all those years ago. And once we recognize this, we discover a parallel universe that's been there all along, moving at a different frequency. A universe where we all exist together, across borders, across oceans, transcending the boundaries of nation and conflict. And in this universe, we're butterflies on fire, each of us finding a new purpose, sometimes alone, sometimes together, that far surpasses that one we carried in the war zone.

A Flat in Kyiv

In a flat in Kyiv, I stand around a folded-out coffee table in a too-small kitchen, where somehow, we've all found a place to raise a variety of Airbnb-provided cups that we've repurposed into shot glasses. I watch Valkyrie stand on a chair, and the youthful brouhaha of the room grows quiet as she begins to speak in Russian to the Ukrainians. But they understand. Because even if they prefer not to speak it, Russian is their first language.

I don't speak either language, but I can feel the words of solidarity before she pours half of her glass of whiskey to the floor by my feet. The others, myself included, follow her lead because I know what they are doing. Honoring the fallen. We've done it many other times, in different flats I've booked throughout the city over the course of a month, where these soldiers and veterans of the war have come together, to congregate, to celebrate, to remember and to forget and to tell war stories among comrades and even myself, a veteran of two other wars, from an Army in a country so far away.

~

The immediate falling into place with them, it was never about which country I came from or for which country I served as a soldier. And those first days in Ukraine, walking the streets of Kyiv, staying up until sunrise on the cobblestone apron of Saint Sophia Square with Alina and Dylan and a bottle of wine, watching Dylan scurry behind women on their way to work with a rose he purchased from an early-morning street vendor—the rose and love he felt in that moment, that we all felt in that moment, it wasn't for the women who blatantly walked by him, head and eyes straight forward to avoid making eye contact while Alina and I watched, laughing. It was about Ukraine and what we all felt there together. Not only with the Ukrainian veterans, but even among ourselves, a group of American veterans from different services and walks of life, just like the veterans in the VA elevator, brought together thousands of miles away from our homes.

We found our parallel universe there, the alternate universe where a coexisting tribe of combat veterans live and breathe, just at a different frequency. The alternate universe that was too scattered and dispersed to find the access point within our own country. But there, in a country still at war, in a population of veterans and soldiers bound together in the face of never-ending war, we were able to live and breathe the air of that world again. We were right back where we used to be, in our own combat zones, free to live without judgment and differences, free to zero in on the simplicities of life surrounding us, just smack-talking and throwing rocks into tin cans. Except this time, in this combat zone we occupied together, we weren't just staying alive, and we weren't sent there to fight for a purpose that wasn't our own. We were there for a purpose that came from within and has stayed with all of us since. And with that shared purpose, we will always be able to find the alternate universe again, no matter where we reside and no matter how far we are from each other.

In the beginning, returning to the United States was a reiteration of returning home from Afghanistan or returning from Iraq. But continuing to stay on, after my American tribe left, allowed me to see war from the outside, to walk the path of transition again alongside those such as Valkyrie, who were given the opportunity to move forward and find a new purpose. And with that, in turn, I've also learned how to return home and walk in the peace life with a full heart. I don't have to fight it anymore, to expect that one day I'll be understood by everyone. I don't have to close myself down in isolation and darkness, and I don't have to try to fit in anywhere, because I know where I belong, and I know where to find my tribe.

Ukraine was my freedom. And in the end, it set me free.

Key Events

Euromaidan Revolution
November 21, 2013–February 22, 2014

The "Euromaidan," or Maidan Uprising, in Ukraine's capital, Kyiv, was a mass demonstration protesting then-President Yanukovych's sudden decision to rescind his promise to sign an agreement with the European Union, and instead to favor even closer ties with Russia. The protests widened as citizens called for an end to regime corruption and the removal of Yanukovych, widely viewed as Putin's puppet. The protests escalated after the violent beatings of unarmed students by Ukraine's riot police, the Berkut (heavily infiltrated and controlled by Moscow), and the regime's passage of anti-protest laws to silence the people. Tens of thousands of ordinary citizens from throughout the country stood side by side, outside, for three winter months, through violent attacks by the Berkut and the government. At the end, when Yanukovych fled to Russia on February 22, 2014, the regime had killed more than 100 private citizens through brutal beatings and the use of live ammunition.

Annexation of Crimea and Insurgency in the Donbas
February–March 2014

Within a week after Yanukovych fled to Russia, the country watched paralyzed as the Russian military seized Crimea's government buildings and held an illegal referendum on Russia's annexation of Crimea. A destabilized Ukrainian government, police force and an ill-prepared armed forces did not react quickly enough, the military having been deprived through years of Russian infiltration and induced corruption. This paved the way for Russia to move forward in implementing a faux "insurgency" in the Donetsk and Luhansk regions of eastern Ukraine, marketing it as a "civil war" with Separatists. It was a breaking point, inspiring a second mass movement of citizens to take action. Thousands of volunteers self-deployed to the East, funded and supported by civil groups' and individuals' donations from around the world, forming an army of volunteers that stopped Russia from further annexation of the country. Thousands of others rushed to enlistment stations to deploy with the Ukrainian Armed Forces (UAF) or National Guard (police force) units. Many of them were turned away, leaving them to self-deploy with the volunteers or seek UAF units with commanders who did not wait for mobilization orders in the midst of the chaos.

Declaration of the Anti-Terrorist Operation
Volunteer Formalization
April—May 2014

As Russian proxies seized government buildings in the Luhansk and Donetsk regions of the Donbas, acting Ukrainian president Oleksandr Turchynov, in lieu of a war declaration, announced the Anti-Terrorist Operation (ATO) on April 13, 2014, encouraging citizens of Ukraine to assist in combating the insurgency.

Newly elected President Petro Poroshenko took office in May 2014, and the state began the process of officially integrating the proclaimed volunteer battalions into the Ministry of Defense (responsible for the UAF) and the Ministry of Internal Affairs (police force/National Guard), although not all volunteer participants were officially documented.

Ceasefire Arrangements
Minsk I September 2014 and Minsk II February 2015

On September 14, 2014, representatives of Ukraine, Russia, the Organization for Security and Cooperation in Europe (OSCE), and the self-proclaimed "Donetsk People's Republic (DPR)" and "Luhansk People's Republic (LPR)," (the Russian-occupied territories of Ukraine), signed the first ceasefire arrangement, the Minsk Protocol. In February 2015, the Minsk-II Accords were signed by representatives of Ukraine, Russia, France, Germany, and the same self-proclaimed DPR and LPR. Both arrangements called for a ceasefire, which Russia violated.

Under the ceasefire arrangements, the Donbas settled into a

violent but static conflict over the next seven years, with no lasting peace and minimal changes in territorial control.

Rebranding of the Anti-Terrorist Operation (ATO) to the Joint Forces Operation (JFO)
April 2018

In April 2018, President Poroshenko placed the Anti-Terrorism Operation under the jurisdiction of the Ministry of Defense and renamed it the Joint Forces Operation (JFO).

Kerch Strait Incident / Ukraine Martial Law Declaration
November 25, 2018

The Russian coast guard fired upon and captured three Ukrainian Navy vessels in the Kerch Strait (international waters) as they attempted to transit from the Black Sea into the Sea of Azov, on their way to the port of Mariupol. In response, Ukrainian President Poroshenko declared Martial Law on November 30, 2018, which expired after 30 days.

Russian Passports Issued to Ukrainians in Occupied Territories
2019–2021

In April and May 2019, Russian President Vladimir Putin signed two decrees to expedite the issuance of Russian passports to Ukrainian citizens in occupied LNR, DNR and Crimea, claiming that it was for humanitarian purposes (for easy international travel for Ukrainians whose passports had expired). By 2021, more than 650,000 Russian passports had been issued to Ukrainian citizens in the occupied territories, which was widely seen as an opportunity to make "new Russians" out of Ukrainians, a preparatory measure for a larger escalation.

Russia's Recognition of the LNR and DPR
February 2022

Russian President Putin aired a televised speech on February 21, 2022, in which he signed a decree recognizing the LNR and DNR, the occupied territories of Ukraine, as independent territories. Hours after the speech, Putin instructed the Ministry of Defense to send Russian troops into the territories for what the Kremlin described as "peacekeeping missions." The following day, on February 22, 2022, Putin declared that the Minsk agreements were "no longer valid."

In another televised address on February 23, 2022, Putin announced a special military operation aimed to demilitarize and "de-Nazify" Ukraine, reiterating an unsubstantiated allegation that Ukrainian forces were carrying out a "genocide" in the LNR and DPR. The following day, on February 24, 2022, Russia launched a full-scale invasion of Ukraine, crossing the border from the north (Belarus), south and east with tanks and ground forces, and unleashing air strikes across the entire country.

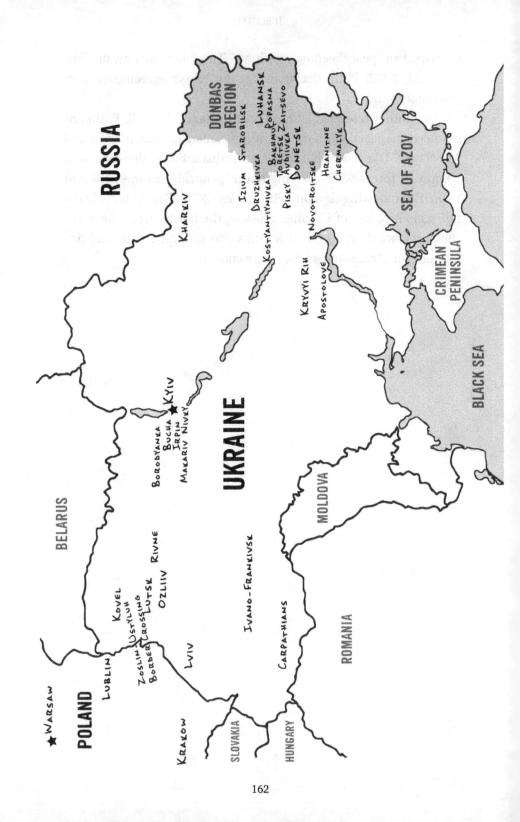

Acknowledgments

THE JOURNEY IN UKRAINE that pushed me to continue writing this more than twenty-year "unfinishable" manuscript (which to be honest, may never feel finished) would not have been possible without the inspiration of the original project and those who made it possible through the language barrier and beyond. The words "thank you" don't carry the weight of how thankful I am to all of you:

Babay and Alina Viatkina, who spent hours of their personal lives orchestrating interviews and sitting at the breakfast table as my volunteer interpreters. Babay, for the emotional and moral support and friendship, for keeping my heart rate up while running to barely catch departing trains. Valkyrie and Babay, for supporting my endeavors to explore the Donbas through a network of camaraderie rather than through hired fixers. Vera Golubkova, Anna Kyselova, and the multitude of volunteers who came forward to bring this project to life; I'm humbled by the hours you dedicated to transcribe and translate more than one hundred hours of oral history recordings. Special thanks to Victor Rud, for your invaluable knowledge and wisdom. Dubas, for bringing me to Valkyrie. John Boerstler and Dylan Tete, who brought Ukraine into my world and continue to support my work there endlessly; thank you for not only this but for the brotherhood and freedom we found in Ukraine together. Phil Butcher, you were also a part of that freedom and support.

There are so many others who supported me along my writing journey that began on journal pages in Afghanistan in early 2002 (many who have read versions of these chapters over the years):

My West Point classmates; comrades and soldiers of the 92nd Engineer Battalion; the crew at the Center for Documentary Studies at Duke. Fulbright Ukraine, who gave me the opportunity to continue my project and continues to support my work in Ukraine. Karen Pavlicin and the team at Elva Resa Publishing, I might have drowned into eternity clutching hundreds of pages of unpublished, scattered thoughts without your encouragement. Thank you for pushing me to see this through.

My dad passed away in 2017. Gone with him, his constant encouragement to never give up on writing, to finish this book that he read the first pages of years ago and continued reading over my years of writer's block and confusion. "How's the book coming along?" was a question he never failed to ask each time I returned to my childhood playground, his writer's office, a museum of typewriters, books, awards, newspaper clippings, and screenplays mixed in with our childhood photos and clay animal figurines carved with my initials to him. I realize now that maybe his passing was an additional force behind my desire to return to war. But by returning to war, I found his voice and inspiration again.

Finally, there are no words to honor the fallen in a world where wars will continue and more will continue to fall. So, to all of Ukraine's revolutionaries, I hope that the words in this memoir not only remain a lasting dedication to all of you, but to all those who fight for change.